Cambridge Elements ≡

Elements in Organization Theory
edited by
Nelson Phillips
Imperial College London
Royston Greenwood
University of Alberta

STARTING POINTS

Intellectual and Institutional Foundations of Organization Theory

Bob Hinings
University of Alberta

Renate E. Meyer
WU Vienna & Copenhagen Business School

CAMBRIDGE
UNIVERSITY PRESS

CAMBRIDGE
UNIVERSITY PRESS

University Printing House, Cambridge CB2 8BS, United Kingdom

One Liberty Plaza, 20th Floor, New York, NY 10006, USA

477 Williamstown Road, Port Melbourne, VIC 3207, Australia

314–321, 3rd Floor, Plot 3, Splendor Forum, Jasola District Centre, New Delhi – 110025, India

79 Anson Road, #06–04/06, Singapore 079906

Cambridge University Press is part of the University of Cambridge.

It furthers the University's mission by disseminating knowledge in the pursuit of education, learning, and research at the highest international levels of excellence.

www.cambridge.org
Information on this title: www.cambridge.org/9781108709323
DOI: 10.1017/9781108671286

First published 2018

A catalogue record for this publication is available from the British Library.

ISBN 978-1-108-70932-3 Paperback
ISSN 2397-947X (online)
ISSN 2514-3859 (print)

Starting Points

Intellectual and Institutional Foundations of Organization Theory

Elements in Organization Theory

DOI: 10.1017/9781108671286
First published online: August 2018

Bob Hinings
University of Alberta

Renate E. Meyer
WU Vienna & Copenhagen Business School

Abstract: This Element reviews the first 120+ years of organization theory, examining its development from the sociology of organizations and management theory. It is initially organized around two streams of thought. The first is found in political economy and the sociology of organizations with an emphasis on understanding the new organizations that arose in the late nineteenth and early twentieth centuries. The second derives from practitioner-scholars whose aim was to provide theories and approaches to managing these new organizations. The Element then shows how each of the streams of understanding and managing came together to produce organization theory. In doing this, it also describes how the institutional frameworks in academic associations, academic centres and journals came out of these approaches and how they strengthened the development of organization theory.

Keywords: organization theory, classical management, sociology of organization, comparative organization analysis, contingency theory

ISBNs: 9781108709323 (PB) 9781108671286 (OC)
ISSNs: 2397-947X (online) 2514-3859 (print)

Contents

1 Introduction

The purpose of this Element is to examine how organization theory began and became institutionalized as a scholarly discipline. The proliferation of large-scale organizations was a characteristic of modern nineteenth- and twentieth-century society (Weber, 1922, 1947; Boulding, 1953; Presthus, 1962; Etzioni, 1964). The Industrial Revolution led to mass production demanding larger and larger workforces, causing mass migration from the country and from agricultural production to industrial production; the factory arrived. With the introduction of public healthcare, the spread of education, movement through railways and automobiles, service organizations appeared and the role of government increased. Throughout the industrializing world, legal frameworks regulating the corporate form (i.e. legal personality, limited liability, transferable shares) emerged. Within the social sciences, notions of 'the organizational society' developed as large-scale, complex organizations emerged in every sector of society. As Parsons (1960: 41) put it, 'the development of organizations is the principal mechanism by which, in a highly differentiated society, it is possible to 'get things done', to achieve goals beyond the reach of the individual.' Initially, the study of social organizations was embedded in and intertwined with the study of developments in society at large. The rise of and subsequent ubiquity of organizations led to the desire and need to understand and manage them as distinct social formations. In fact, 'understanding' and 'managing' are the two streams that produced modern organization theory.

Our aims in the Element are threefold: first, we trace the European and North American origins of the study of organizations located in understanding organizations per se, and managing those organizations. Second, we outline how these two strands came together in the 1950s and 1960s not only through translations of Max Weber's work on bureaucracy but also through the application of open systems theory to organizations. Third, we suggest that knowing where we have come from and the kinds of issues that inspired organization theory can inform our current topics and debates. Early theorists and those who later systematized the study of organizations were confronted with massive changes in society and the kinds of organizations that were delivering goods and services; we argue that this is not much different from the situation organization theorists are facing today. Knowing how our predecessors approached similar issues is not only informative but may inspire a similar productive engagement with organizations.

Discussing the origins of organization theory requires identifying starting points and endings. There are two main starting points – the sociology of organizations and classical management theory. The former is rooted in 'understanding' how the new phenomenon of organizations that penetrated every aspect of society arose and continued to develop and how it impacted society. The latter is rooted in 'managing': dealing with issues of operating these organizations efficiently and effectively.

Initially, the primary location for understanding organizations through sociology was in Europe and drew on the wide-ranging work of the German sociologist Max Weber (1864–1920). His ideas about the increasing rationalization of society, systems of authority and in particular the rational-legal authority system and its instantiation in the organizational form of bureaucracy dominated the discussion. Weber's work was complemented by that of Karl Marx (1818–1883) and Robert Michels (1876–1936), who examined the impact of the bureaucratic form of organization on the power structures of modern societies through ideas of class and elites. Their work has largely shaped the way we think about organizations. Other important sociologists at the time, such as, for example, Georg Simmel (1858–1918), Ferdinand Tönnies (1855–1936) and Emile Durkheim (1858–1917) added influential insights, some of which – like communities, institutions or valuation – have recently seen a revival of scholarly attention.

The term 'bureaucracy' originated in eighteenth-century France and was associated with a common idea of over-regulation and inefficiency in the state (Albrow, 1970). But it was in nineteenth-century Germany that it became associated with the idea of a particular type of administration as well as with a class of bureaucrats. Weber came from this tradition and systematized the idea. His analysis was particularly generative and dominant in the sociological study of organizations leading to an early concentration on the study of bureaucracy (Gouldner, 1954a; Bendix, 1960; Crozier, 1964; Mouzelis, 1967; Mayntz, 1968; Perrow, 1972). Weber's work became part of the North American sociological tradition in the 1950s after the translation of *The Theory of Social and Economic Organization* by Parsons and Henderson in 1947 and *From Max Weber: Essays in Sociology* by Gerth and Mills in 1946. The two strands in this sociological work were, first, elaborating the elements and characteristics of the new organizational form, bureaucracy, that drove and was driven by the increasing rationalization of society (Gerth and Mills, 1946; Weber, 1947) and, second, the impact of such organizations on the elite and class structure of society (Michels, 1911, 1949; Burnham, 1941). We take a broader, more European view of Weber's work than has been the case in much of North American sociology of organizations and organization theory, paying attention to other organizational forms in his work and their place in Weber's analysis of rationalization processes in society.

The second main starting point was a concern with 'managing' organizations. This stream of work became known, retrospectively, as 'classical management theory'. The rise of large-scale organizations posed questions about ensuring that they operated efficiently and effectively. Writers in this genre tended to come from a managerial background and put forward analyses based on their personal insights and experiences (cf. Fayol, 1916, 1949; Follett, 1918, 1924; Urwick, 1944; Taylor, 1947; Barnard, 1948). This was a particularly North American phenomenon spearheaded by Frederick Winslow Taylor (1856–1915), Mary Parker Follett (1868–1933) and Chester Barnard (1886–1961). The emphasis was on issues of planning and strategy, control and coordination of organizational activities. In addition, there were early academics whose emphasis was on the human element in complex organizations (Mayo, 1933; Drucker, 1946). From the Australian Elton Mayo (1880–1949) originated the human relations movement, which morphed into organizational behavior as a scholarly discipline. Vienna-born Peter Drucker (1909–2005) inspired, among many other innovative ideas, an emphasis on management by objectives. A very influential European who contributed to classical management theory was the Frenchman Henri Fayol (1841–1925). While Fayol was working independently of his North American counterparts, he similarly emphasized issues of planning, control and coordination. His work became more widely known with the translation of his 1917 article, 'Administration industrielle et générale' in 1949 as *General and industrial administration*.

When, then, did organization theory emerge as a discipline in its own right? We identify our end point for this Element by the establishment of institutions that recognized, defined and promoted the discipline. In academia, such institutions are of three kinds: the existence of faculties, schools and departments within universities and colleges that have members working on organizational topics; scholarly associations that bring together these scholars; and the establishment of scholarly journals devoted to the emerging discipline.

The existence of business schools is an important marker for engagement with organizations and, eventually, the development of organization theory. Many business schools date back more than 100 years (e.g. the Wharton School, 1881; HEC Paris, 1881; WU Vienna, 1898; Copenhagen Business School, 1907; Harvard Business School, 1908; Kellogg School, 1908; Stockholm School of Economics, 1909), but the real explosion of business schools and, in particular, the study of organizations was a post–Second World War phenomenon. By the late 1960s and the early 1970s, business schools existed in great number, all with faculty members devoted to the study of organizations.

As a result of the increasing engagement with organizations, associations were formed to allow practitioners and scholars to come together and discuss the newly emerging field. In Germany, for example, the practitioner-oriented Zeitschrift für Organisation (*Journal for Organization*) appeared in 1898; the *Association for Organization* (Gesellschaft für Organisation) was founded in 1922. On the scholarly level, in the USA the Academy of Management was key to this development. It was formed in 1936 when 10 professors met in Chicago. By 1960, it had a membership of 387, and by 1970 there were more than 1200 members. A key development occurred in 1969 when the first Divisions and Interest Groups were set up, one of which was Organization and Management Theory. In the UK, Grigor McLelland set up the Society for the Advancement of Management Studies (SAMS) in 1963, signalling the emergence of management and organizations as an important area of study in that country. In Germany, the Academic Association for Business Research (VHB) was founded in 1921; a special section for research on organizations was established only in 1977. Overall, Europe was a little later than North America in forming associations of scholars focusing on the study of organizations. The European Group for Organizational Studies (EGOS) was born in 1973. From the start, EGOS had a rather decentralized structure and worked through a number of Autonomous Working Groups that dealt with specific issues within the study of organizations.

With the existence of scholars carrying out research on organizations and associations for promoting that work, journals emerged, three in particular. In North America, the Graduate School of Business and Public Administration at Cornell University published *Administrative Science Quarterly* beginning in 1957 with James D. Thompson as the editor. In his editorial statement, he said, 'When we look back, in 1966, it may be obvious that administration was at a prescience stage in 1956. Yet if the name of this journal proves to have been premature, it was not lightly chosen. It expresses a belief in the possibility of developing an administrative science and a conviction that progress is being made and will continue' (Thompson, 1957: 1). A year later, in 1958, the *Academy of Management Journal* appeared, although it was many years before it could be recognized as the journal we know today. The third journal was the *Journal of Management Studies*, founded in 1963 as one of the activities of SAMS. *Organization Studies*, the journal of EGOS, did not appear until 1980. Of course, journals have multiplied over the past decades. But by the late 1960s/early 1970s, there was a developed framework of scholars in business schools, scholarly associations and journals which together demonstrated the emergence and institutionalization of organization theory.

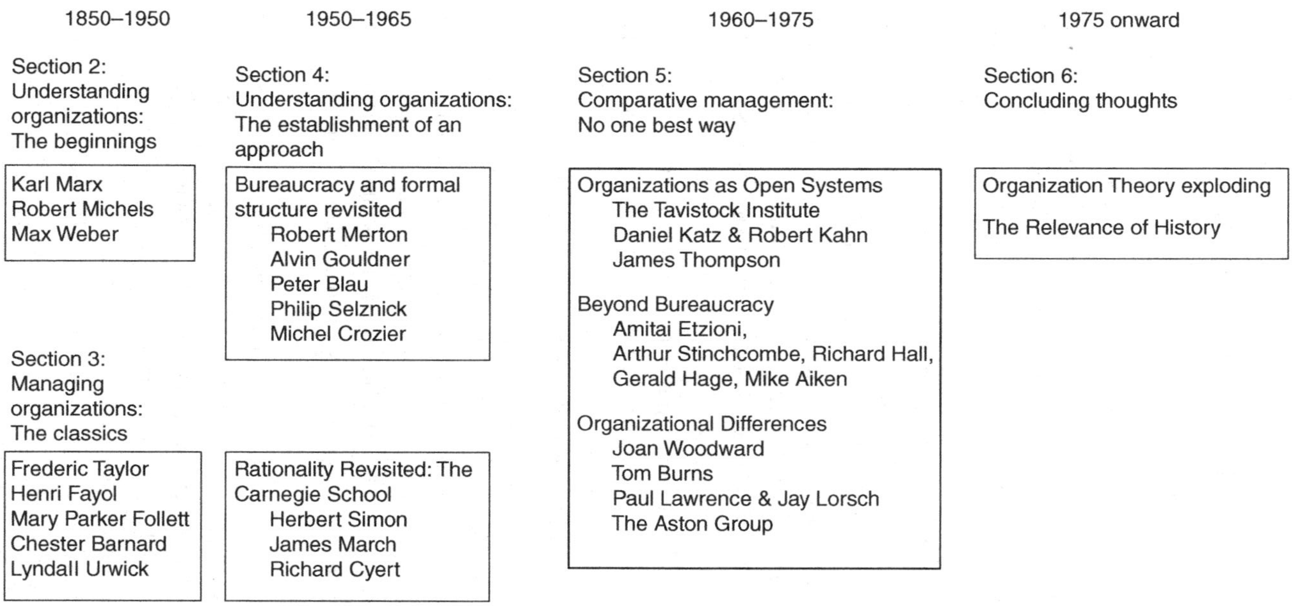

1850–1950

Section 2:
Understanding
organizations:
The beginnings

Karl Marx
Robert Michels
Max Weber

Section 3:
Managing
organizations:
The classics

Frederic Taylor
Henri Fayol
Mary Parker Follett
Chester Barnard
Lyndall Urwick

1950–1965

Section 4:
Understanding organizations:
The establishment of an
approach

Bureaucracy and formal
structure revisited
Robert Merton
Alvin Gouldner
Peter Blau
Philip Selznick
Michel Crozier

Rationality Revisited: The
Carnegie School
Herbert Simon
James March
Richard Cyert

1960–1975

Section 5:
Comparative management:
No one best way

Organizations as Open Systems
The Tavistock Institute
Daniel Katz & Robert Kahn
James Thompson

Beyond Bureaucracy
Amitai Etzioni,
Arthur Stinchcombe, Richard Hall,
Gerald Hage, Mike Aiken

Organizational Differences
Joan Woodward
Tom Burns
Paul Lawrence & Jay Lorsch
The Aston Group

1975 onward

Section 6:
Concluding thoughts

Organization Theory exploding

The Relevance of History

Figure 1 The Structure of the Element

However, there is another strand to this story. The sociology of organizations continued as an important and healthy tradition. Indeed, most of the work on bureaucracy was carried out in sociology departments. The classic North American discussions of bureaucracy (Selznick, 1943; Merton, 1952; Gouldner, 1954a; Blau, 1955, 1956) as well as European ones (Eisenstadt, 1958; Crozier, 1964; Mayntz, 1965) were led by sociologists. The focus of this sociological work was often less on individual organizations than on how society had given rise to organizations as forms of collective action and, recursively, the role formal organizations played in the development of society. With the increasing relevance of organizations for society as a whole and the acknowledgement that society had become not only an 'organized society' but also a 'society of organizations', the study of these new formations became an important area of scholarship.

Soon after the Academy of Management (AoM) had set up divisions, the American Sociological Association, in 1971, also recognized divisions, including one on Occupations and Organizations. In 1959, the International Sociological Association set up Research Committees, one of which covered Industry. In France, Michel Crozier founded the Centre de Sociologie des Organizations in the early 1960s. Even earlier, in 1955, the British Sociological Association began forming special groups, one of the first being Industrial Sociology, which, in Europe, was the main rubric for containing studies of organizations until the late 1970s or even early 1980s. The German Sociological Association, for example, formed a separate section for Organizational Sociology only in 2011.

All of this activity and structural differentiation point to the vibrancy of the study of organizations by sociologists, something that especially came from the importance of Weber as one of the three 'founders' of sociology (the other two being Karl Marx and Emile Durkheim). And indeed, it was initially in the study of bureaucracy that some interests of business school academics came together with those of sociologists.

What this institutional development particularly points to is that by the end of the 1960s, the study of organizations was relatively highly developed in both management and sociology. And, as we will see, for a brief moment the theory of bureaucracy and the study of management cohered around contingency theory and open systems theory. However, by the mid- to late 1970s, organization theory underwent what Donaldson (1995) called 'paradigm proliferation', with strategic choice theory (Child, 1972), population ecology (Hannan and Freeman, 1977), institutional theory (Meyer and Rowan, 1977), resource-dependence (Pfeffer and Salancik, 1978), the theory of the firm (Jensen and Meckling, 1976) and the micro-political approach

(Crozier and Friedberg, 1977/1980). Thus, starting points come to an end by 1970 with the existence of strong research and theory on organizations, professional associations and organizationally focused interest groups and journals where scholars could publish their research. Soon after this, a whole variety of new theories of organizations began to sprout. The coming of age of organization theory had happened.

Figure 1 provides an overview of the Element. Section 2 deals with the origins of organization theory from a sociological perspective, highlighting Marx, Michels and Weber and their concern with how the changing nature of organizations affected and was affected by society. Section 3 looks at the earliest works concerned with managing organizations, the work of practitioner-scholars. These writers were personally involved in managing these new organizational forms. Section 4 takes us forward to the classic studies of the dynamics of bureaucracy where the work of Weber, in particular, was put under scrutiny. At the same time, the idea of organizations as decision-making systems arose, in part, from critiques of the practitioner-scholars, exemplified in the work of the Carnegie School. Section 5 continues the story of systematization with organizations as open systems, the study of organizational differences and the emergence of contingency theory. We conclude in Section 6 by asking the question of 'so what' and suggesting how the history of organization theory should be informative for current issues.

2 Understanding Organizations: The Beginnings

The Industrial Revolution began in Britain in the second half of the eighteenth century and continued through the nineteenth century as it spread across Europe and into North America. The change was the move from an agrarian to an industrial society, from a craft and hand production system to the use of machines within factories to produce large quantities of any product. This transformation required new technologies and production methods (Landes, 1969). Of great importance was the rise of the factory system. Large numbers of people were now in one place, and division of labour, standardization of components and production methods as well as the centralization of decision-making were at the heart of this new way of organizing. The form of the modern manufacturing organization was emerging; by the middle of the nineteenth century, a legal framework for a limited liability company was established in most industrializing countries. Napoleon's Code of Commerce (1806) was at the forefront and provided a template for other countries. In the UK, the Joint Stock Companies Act (1844) and the Limited Liability Act (1855) and in

Germany, the Prussian Corporation Act (1843) provided the legal basis to regulate the new corporate form. This allowed the establishment of the corporation as an organization and actor in its own right, enabling investors to come together to fund larger ventures.

The rise of modern industry brought about many fundamental social and political changes that triggered further organizational change. Apart from the emergence of manufacturing and large-scale factories, there was the development of coal mines, steel plants, trade unions, railways, mass education, higher education, governmental units at both national and local levels, hospitals and so on. All of the new institutions of industrial society produced their own types of organizations, which became ubiquitous throughout the nineteenth century and into the twentieth century. In the twentieth century came the development of more and more services, particularly those grounded in the professions such as accounting, law and healthcare.

We can see this 150-year process summarized in ideas of 'the organizational society', as large-scale, complex organizations became institutionalized in every sector of society. Such organizations were a major characteristic of nineteenth- and twentieth-century society (Marx, 1932, 1965; Weber, 1947; Boulding, 1953; Presthus, 1962; Etzioni, 1964). In the nineteenth and early twentieth centuries, it was sociologists and political scientists who were concerned with understanding the rise of the modern organization and its place in the development of industrial society. Our focus in this section is on Karl Marx, Robert Michels and Max Weber – each of whom was concerned with the ways in which society was transformed and the role that organizations played in that transformation.

Marx and the Rise of Organizations

Karl Marx (1818–1883) was not primarily concerned with organizations per se. His focus was on exploitation, the extraction of surplus value by the dominant class and changing power relations. Nonetheless, his theoretical framework – especially his analyses of capitalist society and its class basis and of the state and its bureaucratic organization – is highly relevant for the early development of organization theory (see Adler [2012] for a contemporary overview of Marx and organizations).

Marx's political economy deals with the dialectic tensions between productive forces (e.g. skills, knowledge, technology, tools and techniques) and relations of production (e.g. ownership relations) and the particular modes of production that characterize societies and historical epochs. Productive forces and relations of production are not abstract concepts but are represented by different social classes – in the capitalist economy these are the bourgeoisie and the proletariat. While productive forces are the motor of development, productive relations materialize the socio-economic structures; the internal contradictions and growing frictions between them give rise to social change.

For Marx, the issue was one of placing the role of organizations, generally, within the social and technological changes taking place in society and, in particular, the impact of these changes on productive processes, class structure and class conflict. As a result, his observations on the topic of organizations are scattered across several of his writings (Marx, 1852/1926; 1867/1959; 1932/1965; 1973). Central is the notion of the capitalist mode of production and the class structure of the bourgeoisie and the proletariat. A concise, short and exciting summary of Marx's thought is to be found in the *Manifesto of the Communist Party* (Marx and Engels, 1848/1955). In Chapter 1, Marx and Engels lay out epochs of history with dominant and subordinate classes culminating in the development and political advance of the bourgeoisie – 'the class of modern capitalists, owners of the means of social production and employers of wage labour' (Marx and Engels, 1955: 51). This dominant capitalist class arose from and was critical to the development of modern industry. Again, to quote Marx and Engels (1955: 54):

> Modern industry has established the world market, for which the discovery of America paved the way. This market has given an immense development to commerce, to navigation, to communication by land. This development has, in its turn, reacted on the extension of industry and in proportion as industry, commerce, navigation, railways extended, in the same proportion the bourgeoisie developed, increased its capital, and pushed into the background every class handed down from the Middle Ages.

As Marx argues, the development of capitalism not only gave rise to the bourgeoisie but also produced the modern working class – the proletariat. Large-scale manufacturing and extensive use of machinery ushered in a division of labour in which the worker becomes an appendage of the machine. Work is divided into simple, repetitive tasks with a drive towards continuous lowering of the costs of production. At the heart of Marx's analysis is the idea of the exploitation of the working class by the dominant class of capitalists through the appropriation of the surplus value produced by workers. The development of the division of labour and hierarchy within organizations is an instrument of control by the ruling class to stabilize and maintain accumulation. Workers create surplus value, as the value of the goods (and services) they produce is greater than the wages they are paid. Capitalists, in Marxian language, appropriate that surplus value. The proletariat become alienated and recognize their exploited position as a result of which, with the help of the vanguard of the working class, revolution takes place moving society to socialism, communism and the withering away of the state (Lenin, 1932). Historically, the Communist Party set itself up in countries such as Russia and China as the vanguard, best representing the interests of the proletariat.

Marx did not analyze organizations as such but focused on social relations of production as the primary source of class stratification and conflict. It is a person's location in the labour system that is critical for his or her class position, and it is tensions between classes that account for the major dynamics of a society. Consequently, it is primarily through the study of labour processes, exploitation and alienation, and the underlying power relations, that Marxist ideas have impacted organization research (cf. Braverman, 1974; Burawoy, 1979; Knights and Willmott, 1990). A dialectical view on organizations (cf. Benson, 1977; Clegg and Dunkerley, 1980) follows the Marxist tradition in focusing attention on how social arrangements bear within themselves the seeds of transformation due to the contradictions and ruptures they inhere (e.g. between forces of production and economic relations). Later, such work folded into critical management theory (Alvesson and Willmott, 1992).

However, Marx addressed organizations directly early in his oeuvre in his critique of Friedrich Hegel's view of the state (which was written in 1843 but not published until 1927). It was in this early work that he devoted attention to bureaucracy. Hegel had argued that the state and its bureaucratic organizational form were independent from the partisan interests of individuals and groups and were concerned with the common good. Marx, in contrast, sharply opposed this conception of state and bureaucracy as autonomous from the two classes, and he contrasted it with his own view of the state as representing the interests of the dominant class, the bourgeoisie, and of bureaucracy as its complaisant instrument. Accepting the idea that bureaucrats could become an autonomous class, with their own interests, would have undermined his analysis of conflict between a dominant and a subordinate class. Indeed, Milovan Djilas (1957) took up this theme as a result of his experiences in the governing Communist Party of Yugoslavia, suggesting that party organization produced a new class: the bureaucratic functionaries.

The importance of Marx to the development of organization theory is not really through his analysis of organizations but through the debates that arose from his work. Marx initiated three important areas of study for organization theory. The first concerns the relationship between societal institutions and organizational forms. The second is related to the analysis of the actual effects of organizational design on workers and the working class. The third highlights relations of power both within organizations and between organizational elites and societal power structures.

These issues relate to what Adler (2015: 134) suggests, 'for scholars in organization studies, Marxist theory has the considerable advantage of embedding the analysis of organizations in a theory of the broader structures of society.' Organizational scholars are urged to see the emergence of particular forms of organization in historical context. As Adler (2015) points out, Marxist theory has made, and continues to make, solid contributions to the analysis of a wide range of organizational forms and their relationship to the nature of labour and class structure (Adler, Kwon and Heckscher, 2008).

Robert Michels and Organizational Elites (the 'Iron Law of Oligarchy')

Robert Michels (1876–1936) was a contemporary of Max Weber with whom he had a friendly relationship until WWI. Michels saw bureaucracy differently from Marx, and in doing so he was inspired by the analyses of elites by Gaetano Mosca (1858–1941) and Vilfredo Pareto (1848–1923). Whereas Mosca and Pareto situated the analysis of bureaucracy in discussions of the state, Michels saw bureaucracy emanating from issues of scale. Organization theory owes to Michels two essential ideas: the first is that bureaucracy is a phenomenon that is not limited to the state but is a feature of all large organizations. The second is that democracy in such large organizations is bound to give way to the rule of elites as power accrues to those at the apex of such organizations.

Size and Structure

For Michels, any large organization develops a bureaucratic form. Because of their scale, involving thousands of members, bureaucratic organizations recruited full-time officials to manage their operations. With the introduction of full-time, salaried managers, organizations develop hierarchical structures with a concentration of decision-making and communication at the top. Scale is also related to the internal and external complexity of problems and functions which in turn reinforce the need for an organization that is both hierarchical and rule based. While this relationship between size and bureaucratic structure was an important observation for the late nineteenth century, it has become a standard finding in organization theory (Donaldson, 2001). But efficiency or effectiveness of formal structure was not Michel's central concern; it was the consequences of bureaucratic structure for internal democracy that was his main contribution.

Hierarchy

Because of the scale and hierarchical structure of modern organizations, Michels suggested that they were necessarily oligarchic. For him, large organizations are undemocratic. Even in organizations whose goals express the importance of internal democracy, such as political parties, trade unions and all kinds of voluntary organizations, the salaried officials (managers) introduce bureaucratic structures to master the increasing complexity that can only be solved through specialist knowledge and training. This unequal distribution of knowledge and expertise, Michels argued, makes participatory, democratic decision-making impossible. Those with power at the apex of the organization become absorbed by the dominant elites and begin to manipulate communications to members and decide policy and strategy to protect the powerful, themselves. This happens even to those who are initially elected representatives of the organization's members.

Like Marx, Michels saw this development as a matter of protecting interests: 'Once in a dominant position, the primary interest of the organization elite is to maintain its power, even if such a policy were detrimental to the organization as a whole' (Mouzelis, 1967: 28). Means subvert ends for the elite to maintain their position. Michel's analysis was based on the rise of mass political parties. In particular, he studied an organization that was supposedly the most democratic: the German Social Democratic party, which was, at the time, the largest socialist party in Europe, but Michels argued that his insights pertain to all types of organizations: for him, the 'iron law of oligarchy' is inevitable, and 'who says organization says oligarchy' (Michels, 1911, 1949). Large-scale organizations are immanently oligarchic, even if this contradicts their very purpose and objectives.

As political activity is impossible without the development of large-scale, powerful organizations, the same oligarchic tendencies pervade the entire society. All popular revolutions lose their way as leaders take over the running of revolutionary organizations, become an oligarchy and instrumentalize the organization to serve their own partisan interests. It is a disillusioned and pessimistic view of the possibilities of change, both organizationally and societally, and it led Michels to give up on his socialist ideals, turn to charismatic leadership, join the Italian fascist party in 1924 and become a follower of Italian Fascism and its leader, Mussolini.

Michels laid the foundation for research on political parties. He has also remained relevant for organization theory not only for highlighting the relation between scale, bureaucracy and power within organizations but also because of his emphasis on the status quo preserving tendencies of large-scale organizations and their impact on the development of society. His work addresses themes of goal displacement and mission drift and how they contribute to the protection of elites. Together, the work of Marx and Michels provides a good background for an introduction to the monumental work of Max Weber, the father of the sociology of organizations.

Max Weber and the Rationalization of Society

Max Weber (1864–1920) studied law and was a professor of economics, but he is regarded as the founder of modern organizational sociology. His engagement with organizations, however, was only a relatively small part in his attempt, like that of Marx and Michels, to understand the historical development of modern society as it emerged and solidified in the nineteenth and early twentieth centuries. Thus, besides his seminal work on *Economy and Society* (1922/ 1978), Weber wrote on *The Protestant Ethic and the Spirit of Capitalism* (1930), *The Theory of Social and Economic Organization* (1947), and *The Sociology of Religion* (1963b). A number of streams to this work continue to be of importance for organization research. One general theme was to go beyond what he saw as the historical determinism of Marx and to elaborate the role of social agency and its meaning in societal and institutional change. Another was to show the way in which understanding cultural ideas, especially religion, was necessary to understand the nature of social institutions and the genealogy of modern society and its economic system. A third theme was to elaborate the systems of domination in societies, and especially to analyze how authority relates to forms of organization. While this last theme is the one that led to an explosion of work on organizations in the 1950s and 1960s, a short account of the other two is necessary to properly locate the wider sweep of Weber's work and also to provide a basis for thinking about how neglected aspects of his analysis might be relevant to contemporary theorizing (cf. Hinings, Greenwood and Meyer, 2018).

Agency and Meaning

In the first theme, Weber was directly challenging Marx's historical determinism. While Weber wrote about this extensively at the theoretical level, his approach is probably best exemplified in *The Protestant Ethic and the Spirit of Capitalism* (1930), a piece that demonstrates Weber's concern with the cultural conditions and especially the impact of religion on the economy. Like Marx, Weber was concerned with the historical question of how capitalism developed from agrarian society via mercantilism and how that shift generated distinctive organizational forms. While Weber accepted that economic factors were at work – such as the development of colonies and early globalization, along with mass production techniques – a critical ingredient was the set of ideas and beliefs within a society and how they inspired people to act in particular ways. With regard to the development of capitalism, Weber saw religious ideas and beliefs as central. In a nutshell, for Weber the Protestant (and especially the Calvinist) belief that a person's earthly success was indicative of whether this person would see salvation in the afterlife led to extraordinary work ethics among believers that drove entrepreneurial behaviour. In addition, the ascetic lifestyle expected from believers prevented them from living in luxury and led to the accumulation of capital. This was quite different from the explanation Marx had offered to account for capital accumulation.

Processes of Rationalization

Weber was a prodigious student of world religions and his thesis concerning the Protestant ethic was developed as a contrast to other major world religions such as Islam, Buddhism and Hinduism in which he saw little or no emphasis on the kinds of work ethics that Protestants thought necessary. This is why he found the Occident in the seventeenth and eighteenth centuries to be the cradle of modern capitalism despite the fact that in many other parts of the world, high cultures and flourishing economies had developed in various epochs in history. In his comparative analyses of societal orders, Weber looked to the dominant belief systems that are characteristic of particular societies. He saw modern societies as differentiated into various 'value spheres' (*Wertsphären*) with distinct ideas, values and established patterns of social action, as well as forms of organizing. In particular, he studied economy, religion, the political sphere, science and arts, and how these spheres interact with one another and, on the societal level, form a configuration. However, Weber did not fall into a macro determinism: value spheres become relevant only inasmuch as actors orient themselves towards them in their actions.

In the development of modern society, Weber saw the main driver in an ever-advancing process of rationalization. Formal rationalization means the increasing relevance of calculative devices and means-ends considerations. For Weber, rationalization is the mechanism that drives development in all value spheres, but substantially, it has different meanings and implications in each of them. For Weber, rationalization plays out at the macro, meso and micro levels. For belief systems or *Weltbilder*, Weber diagnosed a disenchantment of the world, meaning that magic is increasingly giving way to a rationalistic view of the world (the shift from polytheistic religions to monotheistic ones being the first step). The result is a demystification of the world with the rejection of all metaphysical systems of ideas. At the level of organization, bureaucracy becomes the dominant type, colonizing all spheres of life. At the level of persons and their way of life, individualization and an autonomous planning view of actors freed from the bonds of feudalism are in tension with the dehumanizing impact of bureaucracy turning people into cogs in a machine. Capitalism and its bureaucratic organization become an 'iron cage' (Weber's *stahlhartes Gehäuse* is, literally translated, neither a cage nor made of iron, but a casing or shell, hard as steel).

Authority and Organizations

It was Weber's analysis of authority that was the bedrock of his sociology of organizations. Weber, in fact, wrote of 'domination', meaning a situation where the ruler or leader believes s/he has the right to exercise power over others and, importantly, where those in subordinate positions believe it is their duty to obey orders issued by the leader. Weber's concept of *Herrschaft* is sometimes translated as 'imperative coordination'. The central point is that the system of domination is one of authority in the sense that it is legitimate through the acceptance of the relationship between the ruler and the ruled. It is the legitimation of beliefs about the distribution of authority that provides stability in a society or an organization. Weber said, 'the foundation of all authority, and hence of all compliance with orders, is a belief in prestige, which operates to the advantage of the ruler or rulers' (Weber, 1947: 382). He also argued, and demonstrated, that the nature of authority within society changed from historical period to historical period, and the move to an industrial society meant a new and different system of authority, namely, moving away from the traditional and the charismatic to the rational-legal.

Weber asserted that each type of authority system had its own particular organizational form. Authority and imperative coordination are carried out by some form of administrative apparatus that could be sketchy in some organizational forms or highly developed in others. Also, Weber, like Marx and Michels, was interested in the ways in which the system of authority (rational-legal) and its associated bureaucratic form produced a new managerial class. Thus, organizations were important in changing the nature of society by legitimizing such classes and producing new institutional frameworks.

Weber's three authority systems – charisma, tradition and rational-legality – were developed and described as ideal types. He used the tool of an ideal type to bring together the essential and key elements of a particular system and also the organizational form associated with it. Ideal types are analytical devices that, in their pure form, offer criteria against which empirical phenomena can be judged as deviations from the ideal type. As he put it, an ideal type 'is not a description of reality but aims to give unambiguous means of expression to such a description ... it is no hypothesis but rather it offers guidance to the construction of a hypothesis' (Weber, 1963b: 396). Thus, Weber was not expecting to find his ideal types empirically in their pure form nor was he suggesting that all three authority systems could not be found in any particular era or society – an important point that got lost in later discussions.

The first basis of authority is *charisma*. Here, authority is based on the personal qualities of a leader who is seen as set apart from his/her followers. Domination is legitimated for the charismatic leader by his/her extraordinary capacities and abilities. Authority is vested in the person and loyalty is to that person. Typical examples are small-scale, religious organizations such as sects; emergent political parties; or social movements. Historically, this has been seen in Adolf Hitler, in Martin Luther King Jr., in Cesar Chavez and to a certain extent in political leaders such as John F. Kennedy. In all of these, it is often/ usually the founder who claims charismatic characteristics and the authority that comes from them. Of course, many contemporary organizations may have charismatic founders, such as Steve Jobs at Apple, and start-up and emergent organizations may have leaders who have charismatic qualities – for example, Richard Branson when he started Virgin Airlines.

The organizational form that goes with charismatic authority is that of a leader and disciples. Disciples are followers of the leader who have usually been chosen and taught by that leader. Their relationship with the leader is special, and they have the responsibility of mediating between the leader and the wider group of followers as well as those who become interested in learning more. Scale is important, as there may not be enough followers to even require any developed form of organization.

Weber pointed out that charismatic authority is inherently unstable because of its location in an individual and the associated administration is loose and unstable. When a leader dies the issue of succession is probably going to be difficult, as it is unlikely that there will be another charismatic leader. When Steve Jobs announced that he was stepping back from Apple, there was immediate concern because of the belief that he was the organization. With the death or stepping back of the leader, one of two things is likely to happen: one is that there will be extensive infighting between the senior disciples often resulting in the collapse of the movement or, more likely, schism. The other is what Weber termed the *routinization of charisma*. In this situation, the special qualities, or charisms, are passed on to successors through ceremonies and tradition. It is the charisms that are passed on. Examples are to be found in religious organizations, for example, when the Roman Catholic Church elects a pope. The procedures for doing this are well laid out through the College of Cardinals, and the outcome is a new pope who becomes a different person signified by a name change.

A second basis of authority is *tradition* or traditional domination. Legitimacy comes from belief in the appropriateness of established ways of doing things. Precedent, usage, inherited status and custom are the sources of legitimacy. The rights and expectations of various groups in a society are well established by custom and also by an institutional framework that emphasizes established ways of doing things. Particularly important is inherited status, which gives authority in and of itself and establishes domination. Weber wrote of feudal and patrimonial systems with their attendant traditional organization resting on a system of customary rights and duties. Historically, family businesses were organized along such lines.

The organizational form derived from traditional authority is based on both personal retainers – such as relatives and servants (patrimonial systems) – as well as officials who are not personal dependants but are tied by oath to the ruler (feudal systems). While Weber's examples are historical, in modern society generally, ownership and managerial positions can be handed down from parents to children, and a family can dominate an organization for decades. For example, for more than a hundred years, it was not possible to be in a senior position or a member of the board of Cadbury's unless you were a member of the family or married to a family member. Indeed, later scholars have identified the family firm as an example of an organization with an inherited status authority system (Miller and Le Breton-Miller, 2005). Similarly, religious organizations are examples based on custom and precedent, often with roles that represent the routinization of charisma. Interestingly, there has been little analysis of charismatic and traditional authority systems in organization theory generally, although there is considerable study of family business as a relatively specialized area (cf. *Family Business Review*). Similarly, the study of charismatic leadership, per se, has been important, again, in a specialized way (Steyrer, 1998; Aviolo and Yammarino, 2013).

The origins of the sociology of organizations and organization theory are to be found in Weber's third basis of authority: *rational-legal authority.* A belief in law, associated with rationality, is the legitimate basis for this type of domination. Legality means that there are rules and procedures that safeguard both the ruler and the ruled. The power of the ruler is limited by the rules and processes of appointment. Duties and relationships are also specified through legally approved rules and procedures. Both the ruler and the ruled are officials within this system of authority. 'Rationality', according to Weber, comes from the attempt to align means with organizational goals, to carry out rational analysis to achieve organizational purposes. To do so, office holding is based on expertise, and offices have legal authority defined and constrained by policies, rules and procedures.

The form of organization associated with this basis of authority is the bureaucracy. At the heart of the bureaucracy are impersonal rules to guide activities and relationships. In this sense, it represents the depersonalization of authority and action. There are a number of structural elements to a bureaucracy. One is specialization of roles with technically qualified office holders. Another is a clear hierarchy of authority. Specialization and hierarchy are buttressed by policies, rules and procedures which lay down definitions of authority, the distribution of duties and the procedures to be followed for making decisions; at the heart of the organization are written records and files (in the 'bureau') codifying everything. All of this is presaged on the separation of personal and business affairs. In principle, the set of policies, rules and procedures provides for every possible contingency that an organization might face. The bureaucracy is based on a series of contractual obligations, and there is a major emphasis on the impersonal appointment of experts; the bureaucrat follows these rules 'sine ira et studio' (Weber, 1978/1922) – impartially and without affection.

As we will see, Weber's ideal type of bureaucracy became the major starting point for the development of the study of complex organizations in modern society. His argument was that following the advancing rationalization occurring in all areas of society, the bureaucratic form of organizing gradually penetrates all value spheres and institutions of society. Consequently, Weber saw the emergence and spread of large-scale, bureaucratic organizations in the economy, in government, in religion, in education, and in the military.

Weber himself was ambivalent about bureaucracy. On the one hand, he suggested,

> The decisive reason for the advance of bureaucratic organization has always been its purely technical superiority over any other form of organization. The fully developed bureaucratic apparatus compares with other organizations exactly as does the machine with the non-mechanical modes of production. Precision, speed, unambiguity, knowledge of the files, continuity, discretion, unity, strict subordination, reduction of friction and of material and personal costs – these are raised to the optimum point in the strictly bureaucratic administration. (Gerth and Mills, 1946: 214).

On the other hand, he was well aware of the dangers. In a similar vein to Marx, Weber thought the specialization of activities in the bureaucracy produced an incapacity for anyone to grasp the organization as a whole. More generally, he believed that the technical expert was a very limited person in his/her desire for order:

> That the world should know no men but these: it is such an evolution that we are already caught up, and the great question is therefore not how we can promote or hasten it, but what we can oppose to this machinery in order to keep a portion of mankind free from this parceling-out of the soul, from this supreme mastery of the bureaucratic way of life. (Weber, 1924: 414; translation from Bendix, 1977: 464)

Thus, the bureaucratization of the modern world was a potential threat to democracy and the individual freedom that is critical to democracy. The specialized, efficient organization overpowers the individual and limits participation to specified roles. Participation, a key democratic value, is limited by the bureaucratic organizational form.

The relevance of Weber's oeuvre for organization theory can hardly be overestimated. Past decades have brought a resurgence of his thoughts and analyses. Recent crises have brought renewed interest and positive attention to bureaucracy (e.g. du Gay, 2000; Kornberger et al., 2017). Weber's *verstehende Soziologie* forms the basis for the analysis of meanings and meaning structures as well as discussions on 'embedded agency' (Emirbayer and Mische, 1998; Battilana and D'Aunno, 2009). While Weber is not usually claimed as one of the 'fathers' of institutional theory, his emphasis on the cultural and cognitive is instructive. He also strongly influenced Alfed Schütz and his students Peter Berger and Thomas Luckmann whose work became the foundation for neoinstitutional thinking (Meyer, 2008). In addition, rationalization as a motor of societal developments is a core theme in the work of John Meyer (e.g. Bromley and Meyer, 2015). Works on valuation and the calculative imperative (Espeland and Stevens, 1998; Kornberger, Justesen, Anders and Mouritsen, 2015) gain their inspiration from Weber. The overlaps between Weber's concept of value spheres and institutional logics are obvious. But, as we will see, it is his analysis of bureaucracy that produced a vibrant sociology of organizations in the 1950s and that dominated analysis for the 20 years through the mid-1950s, the 1960s and the early 1970s.

Conclusions

Marx, Michels and Weber placed their analysis of organizations within the broad sweep of historical and sociological analyses. They were concerned with the impact of large-scale organizations on the state, on the distribution of power and classes and on society as a whole. These themes – of the state, rationalization, power and class – have been continued by sociologists rather than organization theorists, but even within sociology there has been something of a disconnect between such issues and the study of organizations, and, for several decades, these writers were more or less restricted to the things they wrote explicitly about organizations. More recently, however, with the increasing interest in the role of organizations in society, their broader views have become relevant once again for organization theory. Indeed, *Organization Studies* produced a special issue on the legacy and relevance of Max Weber (Greenwood and Lawrence, 2005). Issues of the emergence of new kinds of organizations and the ways in which they change the state, power, elites and classes are relevant today (Davis, 2016) with the rise of the digital economy. Marx, Michels and Weber should be exemplars of how to deal with these issues.

3 Managing Organizations: The Classics

Marx, Michels and Weber were each concerned with understanding the rise of the modern, complex organization; its role in society; and the ways in which those organizations were structured. All three were academics in their orientation and, in the case of Michels and Weber, for most of their careers. Although Marx was a political activist, most of his writings were academically derived and inspired.

When large-scale organizations were already largely established, a different group of writers focused on how to manage this new organizational form. The increasing scale and complexity of organizations gave rise to questions of how to operate and manage them in an efficient and effective manner. In particular, issues of control and coordination arose, pertaining to relationships between people and machines as well as between people in their new organizational roles. The writers that we review in this section came from technical and managerial backgrounds, their interests and analyses arising from their experience and the personal insights that they gained from managing organizations. The particular writers are Frederick Winslow Taylor, Henri Fayol, Mary Parker Follett, Chester Barnard and Lyndall Urwick. These management scholars came from the USA, UK and France. But also in the rest of Europe management-oriented studies of organizations appeared, for example, in Germany, Eugen Schmalenbach (1873–1955) is regarded as one of the founders of modern business administration.

These writers' emphasis was on issues of the control and coordination of organizational functions and the planning and strategy entailed by such functions. Their understanding was that the capability to manage an organization was not a given talent, but something that could be improved through systematic study and analysis – through 'scientific management'.

Frederick Winslow Taylor and the Measurement of Work

The name of Frederick Winslow Taylor (1856–1915) is synonymous with the term 'scientific management'. He stated, 'scientific management will mean, for the employers and the workmen who adopt it, the elimination of almost all causes for dispute and disagreement between them' (Taylor, 1947: 212). His approach emphasized four key elements: first, the division of labour needs to be efficiently organized. Second, this can be accomplished primarily through time and motion studies that measure work. Third, the shop floor should be the centrepiece of study although the principles can be generalized to all types of work. Fourth, this scientific approach to work will bring together workers and management in a common enterprise, thus eliminating workplace conflict.

Building on these elements, Taylor focused on how to achieve efficiency through the arrangement of work at the shop-floor level and propagated this as an organization-wide system of management. His main writings were *Shop Management* (1903) and *Principles of Scientific Management* (1911). Taylor lived on the East Coast of the United States and, like Fayol, was an engineer by training. Until becoming a consultant, he worked in the steel industry. Two fundamental convictions drove his analysis. One was that management and workers were mutually interdependent and, as a result, the principal objective of management should be to maximize short- and long-term prosperity for workers and management as well as for the owners of the business. However, all around him he saw inefficiency which he believed sprang from antagonism and conflict between management and workers. His second conviction was that the solution to these problems lies in the application of science by which he meant the systematic analysis of work based on measurement – thus, scientific management.

Taylor's approach is distinguishable from the other practitioner-scholars in this section by his emphasis on work and the job rather than the overall design of an organization. His unit of analysis was the task that needed to be accomplished. He emphasized the 'proceduralization' of work together with a specialization of both workers and managers in the tasks at which they were best. Taylor laid down four principles of management in a modern, efficient organization: the first addressed his concern that too much of what passed for organization was based on implicit knowledge and a 'we have always done it this way' attitude. He insisted it was necessary to develop a true science of work that replaced the workers' rule-of-thumb knowledge. This included assigning clearly defined tasks to each worker and setting targets ('a day's work') that were derived from scientific investigation. The second principle involved an appropriate recruitment and selection of people for different jobs, an ongoing performance review and training, with the opportunity for advancement as an additional incentive. Third, constant and intimate cooperation of management and workers was essential. His scientific management required a 'mental revolution' to overcome resistance. It is interesting that Taylor expected more resistance from management than from workers. When reporting on his experiences with organizational change projects, he states that 'nine-tenth of our trouble has been to 'bring' those on the management side to do their fair share of the work and only one-tenth of our trouble has come on the workman's side' (in Pugh, 1985: 159). The fourth principle laid down a strict division between planning and executing tasks and the handing over of all planning and supervisory tasks to a new group of functional managers.

Essentially, Taylor's view of the organization was highly rationalistic, based on the conviction that there was 'a one best way' for dealing with issues of management. The responsibility of management was to find this best solution to issues of performance and productivity through scientific, objective methods. At the heart of Taylor's approach was analysis and planning; Taylor and his scientific management were an almost perfect contemporary example of Weber's Protestant ethic (as a Quaker, Taylor fitted Weber's description) and the increasing calculative rationalization in society. While Weber was very critical of the effects of rationalization on society and Michels bemoaned the unavoidable oligarchic tendencies of large organizations, Taylor was optimistic, and quite utopian, believing that through science could be found the one best way – and that would produce cooperative societies, leading to the end of war!

Scientific management became a movement with its own institutional structure. Taylor first presented his ideas at the American Society of Mechanical Engineers in 1895. Engineers continued to play a major part in the development of scientific management. International Congresses for Scientific Management came into being. For example, the Sixth Congress was held in London in July 1935. The Duke of Kent opened it, and the Prince of Wales spoke in the closing session. Almost 2,000 people attended and more than 200 papers were presented. At the heart of the papers presented was the application of detailed analyses of work, operational planning, cost control and the development of measurement systems to enable maximum efficiency of production, now standard features in organizations.

In addition to the International Congresses, the Taylor Society was created in 1912 by followers of Taylor – such was the power of his ideas. The Society stated that it 'welcomes to membership all who have become convinced that the businessmen of tomorrow must have the engineer-mind'. Among the members were Lyndall Urwick, Frank and Lillian Gilbreth and Henry Gantt. It produced a *Bulletin of the Taylor Society*. In 1936, the Society merged with the Society of Industrial Engineers to form the Society for the Advancement of Management, which continues to this day. A similar society was created in Germany in 1924 (Reichsausschuß für Arbeitszeitermittlung).

Taylor's utopian vision of understanding and cooperation is shown in the following quote:

> A world organization of scientific management could form a right basis for the foundation of world co-operative production and organized sales, removing the economic causes of war. The new philosophy of scientific management must help to bring about the Christian philosophy of love and welfare among all nations. It is absolutely beyond question that a knowledge of the principle of scientific management is fundamental for the success of everybody. (From the records of the International Congress of Scientific Management, quoted in Waldo [1948] and Mouzelis [1967].)

These kinds of sentiments came from the strong belief shared by all the classical practitioner-scholars that large-scale, technology-based organizations were the basis of modern society and that effective management of them was key to both individual and societal health. In spite of these lofty goals, Taylor's ideas have been subject to extensive criticism because of their narrow focus on work and their underlying ideas of motivation and competences. In this sense, 'Taylorism' has become a metaphor for a rationalist, machine-like view of organizations, strict division of tasks, meticulous control and work devoid of meaning. And the introduction of these ideas by Taylor and his followers led to workplace conflict and strikes in many places.

Taylor himself did not see the limitations of applying engineering principles to the analysis of human behaviour, or the rather limited nature of his concept of science. His legacy has been huge, specifically with reference to studies of work and methods and, more generally, to the strongly rationalist basis that he introduced and the continuing importance of rationalist approaches. His contribution to the development of organization theory lies less in his specific ideas about the measurement of work and much more in the idea of a science of management.

Henri Fayol and the Definition of Management

'To manage is to forecast and plan, to organize, to command, to co-ordinate and control' stated the Frenchman Henri Fayol (1841–1925), a mining engineer by training and the chief executive from 1888 to 1918 of Commentry-Fourchambault-Decazeville, a mining and metallurgical company. It was late in his life (1916) that he reflected on his experiences and his *Administration Industrielle et Generale – prevoyance, organization, commandement, coordination, controle* was published. It was not translated into English until 1949 as *General and Industrial Management* (Fayol, 1916; 1949). Like Taylor, Fayol was an engineer who believed that systematic, rational ways of thinking could be applied to organizations to provide more efficient and effective outcomes. Unlike Taylor, he did not analyze the shop floor and production processes but devoted his attention to the whole organization and to management in particular. Fayol's book was very important for the development of organization and management theory: he assigned management its place in the overall operation of organizations by making it one of six functions every organization has to perform; he defined what it is that managers do; and, finally, he summarized his three-decade-long practical experiences with being a manager in a set of 'principles' of management that are still repeated in most textbooks on organization today.

Despite the reference to 'industrial' in the title, it is very clear from Fayol's writing that he believed that the issue of management was central to all forms of organizations, and his aim was to provide a universal theoretical framework. The basis of his thinking was 'functionalism'. He suggested that there were six generic functions that all organizations have to fulfill. He categorized these functions as technical, commercial, financial, security, accounting and managerial (in the original: administrative). *Technical activities* are centred on production, on the manufacture of products or the provision of services. *Commercial activities* deal with buying and selling, keeping the production system supplied and marketing products and services. It is interesting that Fayol distinguishes between *financial activities* and *accounting activities*, just like modern business schools. Finance is about the acquisition and use of capital, whereas accounting deals with balance sheets and costs. The fifth operational function is *security*, ensuring the protection of the organization's property and its people.

As someone who had spent a lifetime managing a large, complex organization, Fayol knew the importance of the sixth function which he labelled *managerial* and expanded into the five key roles which became famous and widely adopted. First, managers have to *forecast and plan*. Organizations need to look ahead and work out plans for future action. Managers are also responsible for *organizing*, ensuring that the enterprise is appropriately structured. A third management activity is to *command*, that is, to ensure that all of the operational and support functions are carried out and maintained. Further, managers are responsible for *coordination*, bringing together disparate but connected activities so that there is unity of purpose and action. Finally, managers have to *control*, ensuring that organizational operations and outcomes are in line with plans and commands as well as the policies and rules of the organization. Fayol believed that good management involved the design and coordination of the other key functions; without management the organization could not work. Fayol's analysis of managerial activities was absolutely unique to him and groundbreaking at the time. Essentially, he defined management through the five key managerial roles.

Fayol also derived 14 principles – 'conditions' on which the working of the organization depended – which he outlined in his book. What is interesting about them is less that several of them have become part of the fundamental canon of management (such as unity of command or unity of direction), but that his reflections about them are not all mechanistic; instead and contrary to Taylor, he states explicitly that organizations are not machines. While the six functions and five managerial tasks are universal, he uses the term 'principles' 'whilst dissociating it from any suggestion of rigidity, for there is nothing rigid or absolute in management affairs' (Fayol, 1949; also in Pugh, 1985: 135). With regard to authority, he not only distinguishes between formal authority that is related to the office and personal authority that is tied to the characteristics of the manager but also highlights the responsibility that comes with authority:

> [R]esponsibility is feared as much as authority is sought after, and fear of responsibility paralyses much initiative and destroys many good qualities. A good leader should possess and infuse into those around him courage to accept responsibility. The best safeguard against abuse of authority and against weakness on the part of a higher manager is personal integrity and particularly high moral character of such manager, and this integrity. It is well known, is conferred neither by election nor ownership. (Fayol, 1949; also in Pugh, 1985: 137)

Fayol's analysis of managerial activities has remained for decades at the centre of discussions of what managers do. Of course they have been subject to criticism, but they have stood the test of time as a theoretical analysis of management activities. Similarly his analysis of organizational functions was an early version of systems theory which became a central element in the formal development of organization theory in the 1960s. His reflections on elements of good management, such as responsibility, integrity, tact and consideration, or equity as a combination of kindliness and justice, have lost nothing of their relevance.

Mary Parker Follett and the Dynamics of Integration

Mary Parker Follett's (1868–1933) background was quite different from that of other classical practitioner-scholars. First, her gender was an issue and she remained one of very few women who were recognized in the newly emerging field of organization studies. While clearly an outstanding scholar, she was refused entrance to Harvard which was then only open to men. She attended the Society for the Collegiate Instruction of Women, known as the Annex, which later became Radcliffe College, and upon graduation she did not become an academic – as was expected because of her strong intellect – but went into social work in Boston, where she was concerned with topics such as youth employment, vocational guidance programmes and building communities. It was because of her interest in vocation and employment that she became involved with industry. Eventually, she became an early management consultant with people from many kinds of organizations seeking her advice. Follett published two books, *The New State* in 1918 and *Creative Experience* in 1924. A collection of papers and essays was published only posthumously (Metcalf and Urwick, 1941), and she has been recognized as an important management theorist by scholars such as Warren Bennis, Peter Drucker, Rosabeth Moss Kanter and Henry Mintzberg. Mary Parker Follett is regarded as a pioneer in organization theory although she never quite achieved the prominence of her male contemporaries. Apart from the gender issue, this may also be due to her being a truly interdisciplinary thinker.

What then were her ideas? Follett was a student of philosophy and political science. She was strongly inspired by pragmatism and a strong advocate of democratic ideas in the workplace. Ansell (2012: 466–67) calls her 'perhaps the most philosophical of classic organization theorists [which] helps us understand both her relative neglect and her periodic revival'. She was very much concerned with coordination, leadership and power. To deal with these issues, Follett turned to the social sciences and, in particular, psychology, which was a relatively new discipline. She thought of organizations as being made up of individuals and groups and the task of management being to understand group processes and to manage those processes so that the purposes of both were served. As with many of the early theorists, Follett believed that the implementation of her ideas would bring about major changes not just in organizations but also more widely in society. The notions of common purposes and common goals for all organizational members were central. At the core of her thinking was the concept of 'partnership'. For her, management in a *democratic society* is about enabling cooperation between organizational members, a cooperation that comes from the willing participation of all.

Follett's analysis showed the key issue in the modern organization as that of coordinating all the parts, but also, importantly, in recognizing that those 'parts' were individuals and groups as well as functions and activities; she added a social dimension to the ideas of Taylor and Fayol. She suggested four fundamental principles of organization, all to do with coordination: coordination as the 'reciprocal relating' of all factors in a situation, coordination in the early stages, coordination by direct contact and coordination as a continuing process.

Building on her philosophical background, she emphasized that all aspects of organizations need to be understood in terms of their relationships to each other. As a result, the basis of coordination is accepting the holistic nature of all the factors in a situation and relating them to one another – 'my key word of organization is relatedness' she noted (Follett, 1942: 259; cited in Ansell, 2012: 258). Her insistence on the situational reciprocal relating of people, groups, activities, functions and the context in which they operate and the dynamics of these relationships are early statements of organizational behaviour, systems theory and contingency theory, and they contain a view on process theories and network approaches. Having pointed out the central issue of coordination of many elements of an organization, Follett then expounded three other principles in which she presented a different version of power, authority and leadership.

One such principle is coordination in the early stages of policy formation, project design and decision-making. She was a very early proponent of participation and empowerment, something which derived from her community-building work as a social worker. For Follett, leadership is not about making decisions and then disseminating them for implementation by others. She believed that participation in decision-making led to higher morale, increased motivation and, thus, better organizational outcomes.

Her principle of coordination by direct contact between group members similarly questioned the role of hierarchy in organizations, emphasizing the importance of horizontal as well as vertical communication. Face-to-face contact is necessary, she argued, that is, direct communication between those people involved to establish a joint understanding of the situation. Hierarchical or functional positions and their presumed entitlements were to be put aside in favour of common organizational ends. Position was much less important than experience and expertise; relevant experience and expertise were to be found in many places within an organization. There is much foreshadowing in her work of the Burns and Stalker (1961) organic organization.

Finally, Follett emphasized that coordination is a continuous process. Contemporary writers such as Pettigrew (1985) and Weick (1979) have suggested that we should think in terms of gerunds rather than nouns. Mary Parker Follett recognized nearly 100 years ago that 'an executive decision is a moment in a process' (1942: 128). She stated that there is no such thing as unity, only the continuous process of unifying. Common purposes, common goals, common action and coordination processes can never be taken for granted; they require ongoing efforts and activities. She suggested that proper leadership was recognizing social, psychological and process issues and especially that management was about enabling collective effort.

With her emphasis on coordination as the central issue for management, Follett brought to the fore the importance of lateral processes in hierarchical organizations. While not using the exact same concepts, she was writing about the integration that was necessary to deal with the differentiation of a complex organization (foreshadowing Lawrence and Lorsch, 1967a). She also suggested a new model of leadership that concentrated on participation, experiences and expertise and the setting aside of hierarchical position, again, a notion that keeps returning in management thoughts. From her political science background and the democratic beliefs which she aimed at bringing into the world of business, she favoured 'power with' rather than 'power over', and joint responsibility for decision-making. Follett also recognized that organizations were based on differences of position, of backgrounds, of experiences, of beliefs, and that coordination was about working with all those differences in a positive manner. She saw that combining disparate elements would produce better outcomes for both the organization and individuals; producing those better solutions could not be achieved through leadership based on domination, or by compromise. Rather, an integrative unity would arise as a creative response to divergent interests and conflicts. Thus, Follett added an important social dimension by applying newer disciplines from the social sciences into the engineering principles of those other analysts.

Chester Barnard and Cooperation

Chester Barnard (1886–1961) was a US business executive who worked for AT&T and served as president of New Jersey Bell for more than 20 years. He was also involved in non-profit organizations and in public administration. During the Great Depression of the 1930s, he directed the New Jersey Relief Administration, which provided jobs and programs for those unable to find work; during World War II, he managed the United Service Organization, providing services to army members and their families. Barnard continued in senior roles after his retirement; he served as president of the Rockefeller

Foundation and as chair of the National Science Foundation. Thus, Barnard had extensive experiences in very different kinds of organizations. He was reflective about his experiences and was invited to lecture at the Lowell Institute in Boston, out of which came his famous book, *The Functions of the Executive* (Barnard, 1938). His collected papers were published in 1948 as *Organization and Management* (Barnard, 1948). Mahoney (2005: 5) praises *The Functions of the Executive* as 'the most high-powered intellectual contribution to organization or economic theory ever written by a practising manager'.

As with Mary Parker Follett, Barnard emphasized the role of cooperation and coordination on which his definition of an organization is based: an organization is 'a system of consciously coordinated activities or forces of two or more persons' (Barnard, 1938: 73). He regarded organizations as complex, organic and evolving systems and emphasized that for an organization to exist, there must be people who communicate with one another, who are willing to commit and contribute to the organization and who recognize and accept the common purpose of that organization. He considers it to be the prime function of the executive (manager) to ensure that these three elements are in place. Barnard also argued that an organization is a cooperative system that is dynamic, in the sense that it operates in a changing environment to which it has to continually adjust. Organizations are part of a larger society; they are 'included in an informal, indefinite, nebulous, and undirected system usually named a 'society' (1938: 79).

Again, as with all of the practitioner-scholars, Barnard started from the assumption that organizations have a purpose, whether that is to produce automobiles, run a railroad, provide social work services or operate an army. If organizations are to persist over long periods of time, their purpose needs to be continuously adapted. To achieve this organizational purpose and the goals that flow from it, the members of the organization must be willing to contribute and cooperate. Like Follett, Barnard argued that cooperation could not be taken for granted and that while a formal organizational structure was necessary, it was not sufficient for producing and coordinating cooperative activities. What is necessary is inculcating the organization's purpose as a belief among members and this is achieved by constant communication. Barnard saw leadership as about communication of what now would be called 'vision' and enabling that purpose/vision to be translated into action. It was essential that members of the organization develop common perceptions of purpose and action. In these ideas we see the seeds of what Martin (2002) calls an integrationist perspective on organizational culture, something that is prevalent among all of the early managerial writers. Their aim was to ensure a purposeful, unified, conflict-less organization.

Barnard was the first writer to emphasize the importance of the informal organization and to examine the interaction between formal and informal. The informal organization arises from interactions that are based on personal interests and issues rather than centred on the common purposes of the organization. But Barnard recognized that such interactions were important for an organization to function. So, he suggested that executives should not only understand the nature of informal organization but also enable that informal organization to be used as an important part of the communication process. Part and parcel of this was his view of authority, one where domination and the exercise of power by executives was seen as counter-productive. Rather, organizational members needed their own sphere of influence where their choices could be exercised. The approach of subordinates and superiors having their own decision-making spheres, he argued, would lead to more effective contributions to common organizational goals. Barnard, with his people-focused view and his elaboration of the informal organization, was in line with the work of the human relations movement (Mayo, 1933). That approach emphasized the existence and importance of informal organization where employees are self-organizing in ways that can be either negative or positive for an organization. Barnard (and others) stressed that the proper acknowledgement of informal relations in the workplace was entirely beneficial for an organization.

Given this cooperative, people-centred view of organizations, what then are the functions of an executive? Similar to both Fayol and Follett, for Barnard they are development, implementation and maintenance of organizational communication; securing essential services from individuals through appointment and retention; and the formulation of purpose and objectives. Understanding and managing the interaction of organizational purposes, organizational functions, organizational structure, informal organization, communication and leadership are critical for management.

Organizational communication is at the heart of cooperative relationships. In emphasizing successful communication of policies, procedures and practices, Barnard sees the informal organization as the most effective channel. By operating through that part of the organization, the need for formal decision-making is reduced. This fits with his view that authority is at its strongest when it does not have to be formally exercised, and that leadership is about ensuring the acceptance of decisions without conflict.

Willingness to contribute is related to the satisfaction that organizational members obtain from the organization. Securing essential services from individuals occurs through emphasis on morale, incentives, supervision, education and training. Hence, Barnard devoted much attention to how organizational members can be incentivized and persuaded to commit themselves to the common purpose. While Barnard recognized the importance of material incentives, he believed that participation, recognition, cooperation and other non-material incentives were more important in obtaining commitment; in all of this, the executive had to be persuasive.

While formulating purpose and objectives is a task for senior management, Barnard was aware that implementation and action on those objectives rest further down the organization. It becomes important that everyone in an organization is cognizant of general purposes and major decisions; only then can the organization be a cohesive whole. Barnard strongly endorsed participation and empowerment. It is not surprising that his thoughts have not only inspired organization theory but have also been highly influential for motivation theories and organizational behavior more generally.

In his conclusions to *The Functions of the Executive*, Barnard (1938: 296) says,

> I believe that the expansion of cooperation and the development of the individual are mutually dependent realities, and that a due proportion or balance between them is a necessary condition of human welfare. Because it is subjective with respect both to a society as a whole and to the individual, what this proportion is I believe science cannot say. It is a question for philosophy and religion.

As with all of the practitioner-scholars, it was Barnard's belief that following a number of principles will make organizations more effective and better places for their members and, at the same time, will bring immense societal benefits. Despite being managers with long experiences in organizations, these writers were also keenly aware of the role of philosophy, and particularly moral philosophy, for the working of organizations.

Lyndall F. Urwick and the Systematization of Management Knowledge

The Englishman Lyndall Urwick (1891–1983) served as an officer in the First World War. His experience in the military was a long-term influence on his thinking about management. After the war, he worked for Rowntree, a chocolate company with progressive leanings. Urwick was involved in the process of modernizing the company and it was through this work that he began to develop his ideas about management in a systematic way. The increasing currency of his ideas led to an appointment as director of the International Management Institute in Geneva. After five years in Geneva, he moved back to the UK to set up a management consulting firm, Urwick, Orr & Partners, which by the 1950s was one of the 'big four' management consultancies in the UK. During Urwick's time, management knowledge was in transition, moving from the ideas of individual thinkers to a more systematic canon of theories of organization. Because of this positioning, Urwick became famous as one of the first synthesizers of existing management thought rather than a producer of novel ideas (Brech, Thompson and Wilson, 2010).

Urwick was a more prolific writer than earlier practitioner-scholars (Urwick, 1944, 1952, 1962, 1956; Urwick and Brech, 1950). The production of so many books and essays resulted from his aim of systematizing previous writers who mostly published one key writing. Urwick was devoted to the ideas of scientific management as put forward by Taylor, to the planning and organizing approach of Fayol, but also to Follett's concepts of leadership.

In embracing scientific management, Urwick reinterpreted some of Taylor's ideas. One of the criticisms against scientific management was that the 'science' in scientific management was no more than a set of techniques. Urwick rejected this critique but went on to broaden the definition, suggesting that scientific management was a way of thinking about how organizations should be managed. First, a commitment to a scientific approach was required, a philosophy which was concerned with the causes of phenomena that could lead to laws of organization. Only after such a conceptual approach could the second aspect come into play, the application of scientific methods of data collection and analyses to make comparisons between organizations, their structures and their systems.

Urwick had a strong conviction that logic should drive the design of organizations, as this would produce both efficiency and effectiveness. He elaborated 'principles', or 'elements', of management, including specialization, authority, definition and correspondence. *Specialization* occurs at both the individual and the departmental levels. For Urwick, the distinction between line and staff was important, with the line ensuring that the production activities of an organization were carried out, and staff being responsible for coordination between these activities. The principle of *authority* demands the existence of a well-developed hierarchy or chain of command. It is necessary for the responsibilities and authority of each position in the hierarchy to be formally *defined*, written down so that all organizational members could understand the workings of that authority. A further important principle is *correspondence* between authority and responsibility of the office holder.

The definition and operation of the organizational authority system was critical for Urwick, who owed much of his thinking about this issue to his experiences in the military where the chain of command is highly formalized. He also recognized that for the authority system to work as intended, leaders must ensure that the purposes of the organization were understood, that actions followed from those purposes and that actions and purposes were consistent. A critical element in producing consistency was forecasting and planning. Urwick emphasized the importance of forecasting because it enables an organization to determine its own path rather than be buffeted by unforeseen events; planning ensures that an organization is able to carry out the activities that are necessary for effective performance.

Given the volume of his writing, there was little in the operation of organizations on which Urwick did not comment. He systematized and extended the work of Taylor and Fayol, believing strongly in their logical, structural-functionalist approaches to the management of organizations. Together with Luther Gulick (1892–1993), Urwick developed the acronym POSDCORB, meaning Planning, Organizing, Staffing, Directing, Coordinating, Reporting and Budgeting (Gulick and Urwick, 1937). He also gave recognition to Follett's ideas about participation and leadership. But this aspect of his work was taken up more systematically by his collaborator Edward Brech (1909–2006), who emphasized the social character of management and the importance of motivation and participation (Brech, 1969).

Urwick played an important role in establishing an institutional framework for management education in the UK. After his service in World War II, he was involved in several initiatives, including chairing the Education Committee of the Institute of Industrial Administration, the Committee on Education for Management of the Ministry of Education and the Education Committee of the British Institute of Management. Mirroring his mission to systematize management knowledge within organizations, Urwick saw the need for systematic management education in the UK at a time when it did not exist in higher education. He became strongly involved with the establishment of the Administrative Staff College at Henley (now the Henley Business School) and with the British Institute of Management, founded in 1948, for which he wrote 'a blueprint for the future'. For several decades, Urwick was in demand as a consultant, and he played an important role in establishing management consulting as a recognizable profession. His belief in a scientific and systematic approach to management meant that he was strongly committed to building the institutions of education and accreditation that would ensure appropriate training for managers.

Conclusions

Taken together, these writers exemplify the attempt by practitioner-scholars, over a period of approximately 60 years, to develop a systematic basis for managing organizations. Their aim was to conceptualize organizations as purposeful with the role of management being to design structures and systems of activities and to coordinate those interrelated activities and functions through planning, goal setting, coordinating, performance management and leadership. This was to be achieved through the application of rational, logical – 'scientific' – approaches that would lead to extensive cooperation within the organization resulting in superior performance. An underlying idea was that the application of scientific principles and rigorous analyses would contribute to progress. While primarily based in the managerial experiences of the writers, their analyses were quite abstract and primarily functional in form. They sought to distil experience to produce principles of organizational design and management that are universal. Because of their belief in such principles, Mouzelis (1967) refers to them as the 'universalist' school. Above all else, they wished to improve the practice of management based on their conviction that organizations were so important that their effective management would alter the nature of society.

The approaches and ideas described in this section became known as 'classical management theory': 'classical' because of the historical origins and longevity, 'management' because of the emphasis on efficient and effective ways of managing organizations, 'theory' because of the attempt at systematization of experiences into principles and elements. By the 1930s and 1940s, classical management theory was established, specifying how organizations could be better managed, identifying the role and functions of management and enumerating principles of administration. There was much interest in the design of formal organizational structures with the belief that through structures both operational and support activities could be performed with certainty.

For classical management theorists, good management was a matter of sound organizational design with supporting policies and rules. Essentially, the organization was regarded as a closed system of interdependent structural features. While there were references to the impact of external factors, these could be dealt with through good forecasting and planning, and real attention was to be given to organizational design. Of course, while Follett and Barnard did give considerable emphasis to cooperation, communication and leadership, it was within a framework of sound organizational structures as a necessary part of achieving organizational goals.

Institutionally, the development of organizational theories that were meant to lead to better management practice had two effects. One was the development of management consulting; the other was the legitimation of management education.

The journey from Taylor to Urwick illustrates the development of management consulting during this time. Taylor himself was a consultant, starting a practice in 1893. Not long before that, in 1886, Arthur D. Little was founded and became one of the leading consulting firms of the twentieth century. The next period of growth was in the 1930s and management consultancy took off after World War II. So, for example, Urwick, Orr & Partners was set up in the early 1930s and by the 1950s it was one of the most prominent consulting firms in the UK. It was the development of large-scale organizations and the greater understanding of how they operated that was provided by these early writers that enabled management consulting to appear and proliferate (McKenna, 2006).

Producing analyses that purported to show how to design organizations that would be more productive, more efficient and more effective produced a desire to disseminate those ideas through formal education as well as through consultancies. In North America, in particular, the rise of the business school followed the trajectory of the evolution of large-scale organizations. Barnard and Follett had strong associations with universities and both gave lecture series on management. Urwick, as we have seen, was instrumental in establishing the first major business-oriented college in the UK and in all of the post-war discussions of management education in the UK. He was also prominent in similar discussions in the USA.

By 1950, increasingly systematic ideas about how to manage the new organizations were being established together with a developing institutional framework for the promulgation of those ideas through consultancy and management education. What, then, did the 1950s and 1960s hold for the development of organization theory?

4 Understanding Organizations: The Establishment of an Approach

In Sections 2 and 3, we described early work on organizations. One stream, rooted in sociology and the work of Max Weber, emphasized the ideas of the rationalization of the modern world and the spread of bureaucratic organizations. This approach was academic in tone as scholars attempted to understand what was happening in society and how the newly emerging organizations fitted into these developments. The analysis of organizations, per se, intersected with analyses of society, class, power and authority. The organization was placed within its societal context.

The second stream, classical management, was the work of practitioner-scholars who wanted to make sense of the organizations in which they worked; their emphasis was on principles of organizational design, processes of cooperation, the specialization of work and technology. Their aim was to build organizations that would be efficient and effective, producing greater wealth for everyone. There was a utopian streak to these analysts, as they believed that appropriately designed and managed organizations would lead to harmonious societies.

From approximately 1940 to the end of the 1950s, these streams remained relatively separate. In both, scholars of organizations wrestled with the legacies of the founders, in particular with their emphases on the formal organization, especially formal structure, and on the rationality and efficiency of the bureaucratic form. The study of bureaucracy remained central to the sociology of organizations but with a focus on informal structures and the internal dynamics of bureaucracy; an inward focus developed, thereby moving away from the diagnosis of organizations in society. The classical management approach was transformed as its ideas were taken over by academics and subjected to more rigorous analysis. In a related way, theory developed that focused on organizations as systems of decision-making and on the limits of rationality. In all of this, the study of organizations began to look inwards and move away from a diagnosis of the organization's role in society.

At the end of 1950s, the study of bureaucracy began to morph into what has been labelled 'comparative management theory', culminating in what was to become the dominant approach to organizational analysis, namely, 'structural-contingency theory' (Van de Ven et al., 2013). This approach that dominated organizational research for almost 20 years was but a brief moment in the study of organizations! More on this in Section 5; in this section, we continue the story of how research on understanding organizations developed immediately after World War II.

The Sociology of Organizations: Bureaucracy and Formal Structure Revisited

The discussion of organizations in English-language sociology saw a major change with two translations of Max Weber's work: one was by Hans Gerth and C. Wright Mills, *From Max Weber: Essays in Sociology* (1946). The other was the translation by Talcott Parsons and Alexander Henderson of Weber's *The Theory of Social and Economic Organization* in 1947. Both dealt with work published in German 25 or more years earlier. But of course, bureaucracy had already been the focus of the sociology of organizations before these translations; consequently, while both volumes covered much of Weber's sociological analysis in general, such as on power, religion, social structure, social action, methodological stance, it was his writing on patterns of authority and bureaucracy that had become central for the sociology of organizations.

The emphasis was on applying Weber's work empirically and exploring whether the bureaucratic organization worked the way Weber was presumed to have outlined. Robert Merton (1910–2003), who had been a student of Talcott Parsons at Harvard, created a 'hub' for research on bureaucracy at Columbia University, which became a central player in the establishment of North American sociology. Merton was a theorist of structural- functionalism but promoted a 'softened' version by highlighting concepts such as functional equivalents, latent functions, unanticipated consequences or dysfunctions. He wrote extensively on these topics (Merton, 1936, 1940, 1949) and produced the edited volume *Reader in Bureaucracy* (Merton, Gray, Hockey and Selvin, 1952) which brought together a wide range of classical writings on bureaucracy for the first time. Merton favoured middle-range theories. He emphasized the desirability of connecting theory to systematic empirical observation, influenced by his friend and colleague at Columbia, the Austrian emigrant Paul Lazarsfeld. Merton had three students in particular who dealt with the issues of bureaucracy in their PhD theses and exemplified this approach: Alvin Gouldner, Peter Blau, and Philip Selznick.

Weber was, of course, German as were Marx and Michels. Methodologically, Weber is the founder of *verstehende* sociology emphasizing meaning and cultural embeddedness (Weber, 1947). However, the reading that English-speaking organizational sociologists, in general, and in the USA in particular, took from Weber's work was a view of bureaucracy as formal organization structure, emphasizing causal explanation and rationality. This formality was to be found in the central and defining components of a bureaucracy – specialization of functions and activities based on technical competence; impersonal and written rules that laid down authority, roles, relationships and activities; and authority distributed on the basis of role, both in terms of specialization and level in the hierarchy of office.

The bureaucratic organizational form represented the separation of the official and public from the personal and private. Relationships in a bureaucracy are contractual, and expertise is at the heart of organizational operation. With such an organization, the ultimate in efficiency and effectiveness could be achieved. Essentially, a bureaucracy is presented, in this interpretation of Weber, as a machine-like, depersonalized setting. Weber's own critical view of bureaucracy and its technical experts disappeared; the bureaucrat who operates *sine ira et studio* and the ideal type of bureaucracy had been mistaken for descriptions of empirical reality or at least as normative and desirable features of rational organization design. While, more recently, there has been criticism of this limited view of Weber's analyses, it was this interpretation that drove English-speaking organizational sociology for two decades. In the German-speaking world, interestingly, a middle-range sociology of organizations did not develop until, in the 1960s, English research on organizations started to 'infiltrate'; the pioneers were Renate Mayntz (1963, 1968) and Niklas Luhmann (1964). Essentially, the sociology of organizations accepted the basic bureaucratic thesis that this form of organization was indicative of the modern world as it moved to larger-scale production and the depersonalization of society (Scott and Davis, 2011).

The idea of a distinction between formal and informal structure had already been recognized through the work of the human relations move-ment (Mayo, 1933; Roethlisberger and Dickson, 1939). Its descriptions of formal organization, emphasizing rules and procedures, clear authority systems and the division of labour, looked remarkably like the concept of bureaucracy. The diagrammatic way of capturing much of formal organiza-tion is through the organization chart. The concept of informal organization recognized that much that happens in organizations is emergent and follows formal prescriptions only to a rather limited extent. Contrary to being harmful for overall goal achievement, it was often found to be the informal practices, politics and social networks that enabled organizational opera-tions to proceed because, on the one hand, it is never possible to specify every aspect of roles and authorities and, on the other hand, there are different patterns of values and interests among organizational incumbents. In this human relations tradition, studies showed that the actual roles and relationships within formal organizations were problematic (Dalton, 1950, 1959; Roy, 1952) – for both managers and workers, rules were subverted, roles were altered and relationships could be antagonistic.

Merton and his students took up these ideas with their studies of the internal workings of bureaucracy. They were exploring whether the image of bureau-cracy as an efficient, mechanical system of roles would stand the test of empirical scrutiny. Weber himself had emphasized that his ideal-type theoriz-ing was a device for summarizing key characteristics, providing a backdrop against which empirical phenomena could be judged as more or less compliant with the model. Merton and his students took the concept of bureaucracy as a 'real' type and questioned and examined the actual operation of bureaucratic organizations to see how 'ideal' the ideal type was. Given the importance of informal features of organizations, they aimed at showing that it was impos-sible for a bureaucracy to be as it was thought Weber had outlined.

Alvin Gouldner and Three Patterns of Bureaucracy

For Alvin Gouldner (1920–1980), the main question was how a new organizational form, the bureaucracy, could gain legitimacy in the face of conflict and resistance, thereby challenging the notion of bureaucratic organizations as rational entities pursuing one shared goal. He was critical of Weber's ideal types, stressing that they did not help understanding what was actually going on in organizations. His own study of a gypsum mine in the USA (Gouldner, 1954a) examined, in detail, the way in which rules and commands were applied and obeyed (or not). The pre-bureaucracy management system of the mine worked on the basis of what Gouldner described as an 'indulgency pattern': there was a relaxed approach to supervision, rules were sometimes ignored or applied in a very lenient way, deviation from the formal rules was tolerated; the mine was well integrated into the community. In exchange, there were very few conflicts, the workers trusted their superiors and were highly committed to the organization, which manifested, for example, in their willingness to do overtime if necessary. Into this situation came the new mine manager with a mission to increase output. As the informal relations of the old manager were not available to him, he resorted to formal structures and aimed at completing his mission by introducing bureaucracy, an efficient, rational-legal organization. With this organizational change, Gouldner observed conflict, morale issues and the problematic nature of rules and goals. Indeed, such was the conflict that he published a second book from this case, *Wildcat Strike* (Gouldner, 1954b).

As a student of Merton, Gouldner was familiar with the distinction between anticipated and unanticipated consequences of action and the notion of latent functions. Gouldner's interpretation was that Weber's ideal type of bureaucracy and Parson's functionalism had failed to pay attention to both and overlooked that different parts of the organization are often pursuing quite different, and sometimes conflicting, goals. Given the centrality of rationality in theories of bureaucracies, Gouldner raised the question: 'rational for whom?' His study of the gypsum mine led him to postulate three patterns of bureaucracy, namely, 'mock', 'representative' and 'punishment centred'. Gouldner emphasized that these three are not mutually exclusive, but that organizations are complex social systems where multiple modes may be at work to different degrees at the same time.

In a *mock bureaucracy*, rules are prescribed by an outside agency, for example, an insurance company or corporate headquarters, but the majority of organizational members see them as illegitimate. As a result, they are rarely enforced unless a representative of the outside agency is present. There is a decoupling of rules and actions, and since workers and management are in agreement, conflicts are low and morale is high. *Representative bureaucracy* occurs where organizational members whose authority is regarded as legitimate produce the rules. In effect, this is the ideal-type Weberian situation where rules are obeyed because of the role of legitimate experts with an emphasis on technical efficiency. This type of bureaucracy fits with the ideas of classical management writers' (e.g. Fayol and Follett) idea of harmonious collaboration. Gouldner found representative bureaucracy to be at work, for instance, with safety rules. *Punishment-centered bureaucracy* occurs where one group imposes a set of rules on another group and coercion is at the root of compliance. Rules and the surveillance and sanctions that are necessary to enforce them provoke resistance which triggers additional rules and surveillance. Quite contrary to the view that rules and their enforcement produce order and stability, this spiral eventually destabilized the system. It was this bureaucratic mode – which Gouldner regards as the incarnation of Weber's iron cage – that was introduced into the gypsum mine and eventually led to a wildcat strike.

Gouldner raised important questions about organizations following up on the idea of unanticipated consequences and asking who actually benefits from formal bureaucratic organizations. In his *Patterns*, and also in his later more general theorizing (Gouldner, 1970), Gouldner was questioning the Weberian idea of organizations as goal-oriented, rational instruments. For him, organizations served particular interests and were sites of conflict between different groups seeking to establish control. For Gouldner, consensus is unusual; conflict is the norm.

Peter Blau and the Dynamics of Bureaucracy

In *The Dynamics of Bureaucracy* (Blau, 1955), Vienna-born Peter Blau (1918–2002) presents a more positive view of bureaucracy, both in terms of its day-to-day operation and its ability to deal with change. However, for him the critical component is the informal organization as expressed through the social interaction of organizational members. Indeed, the subtitle of the book is 'A Study of Interpersonal Relations'. Blau carried out a comparative case analysis of a state employment agency and a federal law enforcement agency showing that much of what actually went on in the organization followed informal channels with organizational members carrying out activities that were not part of their prescribed job descriptions. He discussed how these activities had a latent functionality and contributed to the productivity of the organization. In line with the Hawthorne studies (Roethlisberger and Dickson, 1939), Blau primarily identified the informal organization as positively supporting organizational tasks and outcomes. Thus, there were both formal and informal mechanisms of control, adaptation and change. His empirical study led him to the conclusion that bureaucracies are not static, unchangeable organizations as was believed to be Weber's legacy. Instead, Blau argued that bureaucracies are dynamic structures, particularly through the informal organization, a flexible source of change. However, he also identified dynamics that were more detrimental, including too much adherence to rules in and of themselves. Such adherence led to rigidity in decision-making and operations. Also, goals could become displaced through these rigidities.

In developing his view, Blau highlighted informal processes as necessary components of bureaucratic operation *and* the socio-emotional exchanges that take place in organizations. A further part of his argument was the role of status systems and power. Although Blau was examining government bureaucracies, he made the general argument that informal power networks and status systems are generic to all organizations and that it is through these networks of interaction and exchange that organizational members gain access to resources. He showed that informal status differentiation introduced differences in authority among those who are formally equals and undermined the legitimacy of the formal hierarchy. Blau's study on the dynamic workings of bureaucracy and the positive role that informal activities and relationships play was highly insightful and influential, widening the discussion of bureaucracy.

Later in his career, Blau (1964) focused more on exchange relations and moved away from qualitative case studies to a deductive, quantitative approach to study the interrelationship between multiple components of bureaucracy by comparing large numbers of organizations. Blau and Schoenherr (1971) studied the effect of size and scaling on organizational structures and contributed to comparative organization research.

Philip Selznick and Organizations as Recalcitrant Tools

Philip Selznick (1919–2010) was studying with Robert Merton and writing before either Gouldner or Blau, but we portray him as the last of the Merton students because his work is still frequently used in organizational research and has more recently seen a revival (Kraatz and Flores, 2015).

Selznick published on bureaucracy before the translations of Weber's work became widely available in the English language. His article in the *American Sociological Review* 'An approach to the theory of bureaucracy' (Selznick, 1943) drew directly on Weber's work in the original German. In this article and in his later 'Foundations of the theory of organization' (Selznick, 1948), Selznick saw bureaucracy as a special case within a general theory of organizations. In both articles he drew on the work of Barnard (1938) as well as Roethlisberger and Dickson (1939), Urwick (1944) and especially Michels' (1911) iron law of oligarchy. Thus, Selznick spanned both the sociological and the classical management approaches to understanding organizations. Selznick, then, became a link between the concern with Weberian bureaucracy, per se, and the development of a broader sociological theory of organizations. Finally, with his observation that some organizations become institutions, he was a core representative of the so-called old institutionalism (Powell and DiMaggio, 1991; Selznick, 1996) and a link to institutional theory.

Selznick's classic research on the Tennessee Valley Authority, *TVA and the Grass Roots* (Selznick, 1949) was not directly a study of bureaucracy in the same sense as the work of Gouldner and Blau, but it was a study of the dynamics of a large-scale organization. As with his sociological contemporaries, Selznick wanted to show that the rational, purposive view of organizations needed to be extended and critiqued. A key distinction he proposes is between an organization as 'the structural expression of rational action' (Selznick, 1948: 25) and an organization as an adaptive social structure where the 'non-rational' aspects of behaviour are important. For Selznick it was crucial that the 'non-rational' or more accurately, the informal social structure of an organization, remains 'at once indispensable to the continued existence of the system of coordination and at the same time the source of friction, dilemma, doubt and ruin' (Selznick, 1948: 25). As Kraatz (2009: 62) puts it, Selznick 'exposed a sort of hidden world within organizations and showed that they were recalcitrant tools that often failed to fulfil their official purposes or serve their intended constituencies'. What is more, they can be hijacked by partisan interests, a theme that he analyzed in a study of the Communist Party which he tellingly called *The Organizational Weapon* (1952).

An important point here is that while organizations have formal purposes and goals, internal and external constituencies attempt to prioritize their own interests and their own views of organizational purposes. TVA was a government-owned agency with a quite extensive portfolio: producing electricity, developing waterways, controlling flooding, preserving forests, producing fertilizers and more generally developing the rural farming area. Its range of activities spanned multiple states. The TVA had the task to be integrative and participative with an explicit aim of stimulating local participation in its policies and operations (hence the subtitle 'and the grassroots'). The TVA chose a model of integration through a decentralized decision-making style and the co-optation of local groups into its decision-making bodies. However, as a creature of the New Deal in the USA, it faced opposition on various levels, particularly from local interests in agriculture. Those local interests were well organized and the TVA came under intense pressure to divert from its stated purposes and to respond more directly to the concerns of such organized interests. Selznick focused on the ways in which the adaptations that took place changed the character and purpose of the TVA. He showed how the mechanisms designed to put the objective of integration into action actually thwarted democratic participation and the fulfilment of the organization's goals.

Selznick is highlighting that organizations are continually involved in struggles to win consent and legitimacy for their existence, their purposes and their goals with both internal and external groups. To articulate this point, he discusses co-optation, the mechanism the TVA used to acquire consent. Selznick (1949: 34) defines co-optation as 'the process of absorbing new elements into the leadership or policy-determining structure of an organization as a means of averting threats to its stability or existence'. This means co-optation is about dealing with potential supporters and adversaries by bringing them into the organization in the hope of producing positive attachments to the organization.

Like the other Merton students, Selznick was interested in the differences between the formal and the informal, and he highlighted that co-optation can be both formal and informal. With *formal co-optation* (e.g. by having representatives on boards and councils, or by keeping people at arm's-length through advisory groups), Selznick (1949: 34) observed that 'what is shared is the responsibility for power rather than power itself.' As part of the formal organization, this sharing is visible for all to see, and it publicly demonstrates that the organization is dealing with specific interests. Such co-optation is a means of deflecting pressures from less powerful interest groups. Selznick concludes that formal co-optation is often 'the sharing of public symbols or administrative burdens of authority and public responsibility, but without an actual transfer of power' (1949: 260). Such actual transfer occurred through *informal co-optation* of external constituencies who were pushing their particular interests, resulting in a subversion of the original TVA goals of being a democratic, decentralized and inclusive organization. While co-optation is an adaptive mechanism aimed at securing legitimacy, through the actual sharing of power with partisan interest groups the grass-roots idea became a protective ideology.

Selznick developed a view of organizations as cooperative endeavours but showed that by having to accommodate interests of both internal and external groups in their operations, organizations are subject to pressures that deflect and even replace formal and legitimate goals. He also drew attention to the role of the environment in structuring organizations, but he did not conceptualize the environment as a set of abstract dimensions, but as constituencies and groups of actors with their particular interests and a wish to influence and direct the organization. As Selznick (1957: 42) put it, 'we look beyond the formal aspects to examine the commitments that have been accepted in the course of adaptation to internal and external pressures.'[1] His view on the power struggles inside and outside the organization is an important early contribution to a more political view on organizations, a perspective that was at the centre of the next scholar we introduce.

Michel Crozier and the Vicious Cycle of Bureaucracy

In his early career, the Frenchman Michel Crozier (1922–2013) had been drawn to Marxist and existentialist thinking and, accordingly, in his early research he asked why office workers were not more class-conscious (Friedberg, 2009). In 1952, Crozier had joined the Centre National de la Recherche Scientifique (CNRS) in Paris and conducted several case studies of factories which were part of the French public tobacco monopoly, various clerical agencies both public and private, a ministry and insurance companies. Two of these case studies became the basis of his famous study on *The Bureaucratic Phenomenon* (1963/1964). During these studies, he turned away from Marxist macro-sociological, class structural explanations and focused on organizations as levels of analysis. He had spent a year at the Center for Advanced Study in the Behavioral Sciences at Palo Alto in 1959 where he completed the draft of his book; he had already visited the USA several times and been in contact with the work of organizational researchers there. It was this time of intellectual ferment that enabled Crozier to produce *The Bureaucratic Phenomenon* which developed his key ideas about the study of organizations (for an excellent account of Crozier's intellectual history, see Gremion, 1992).

Similar to the work of the Columbia researchers on bureaucracy, Crozier was challenging the rationality and formal structure of bureaucratic organizations and the link to efficiency. In addition, Crozier drew on Dahl's (1957) theories of power; Dahl regarded power as relational and emphasized the dependencies between the actors involved, and on the work of the Carnegie group on the bounded rationality of organizational actors (see later).

---

[1] For a fuller treatment of Selznick's approach to organizations and to sociology see Hinings and Greenwood (2015), Hinings, Greenwood and Meyer (2018) and Kraatz (2015).

Central to Crozier's thinking about organizations were the issues of uncertainty, power, agency and the difficulties of organizational and social change. From his empirical studies, he derived four central observations: first, he found that the enormous number of formal rules constrains all actors in the system, but at the same time it gives them autonomy as they can always fall back to the rules (the literal 'work to rule' as a form of resistance) and the rules also bind the superior level. This leads, second, to a centralization of decision-making, as rules can never prescribe all eventualities and only higher levels can make exceptions from the rules. This implies that decisions have to be taken at levels that are not close enough to the action to have all necessary insights. Third, the strict hierarchical system entails a stratification of highly cohesive groups and departments which makes groupthink and goal displacement an almost necessary consequence. Finally, fourth, again relating to the necessary incompleteness of rules, power relations parallel to the ones foreseen in the hierarchy evolve around the control of the remaining uncertainties. He shows this with the example of the maintenance mechanics in the tobacco factory (the 'industrial monopoly' as Crozier calls it). As bureaucratic rules regulated work relationships in meticulous detail, the key source of uncertainty in the plant was machine breakdown, an uncertainty these mechanics controlled and which gave them power and the ability to promote their own interests. Crozier holds that 'the more narrowly the organization is regulated, the greater the independence of the experts' (1964: 193). Hence, these zones of uncertainty become the centre of informal power struggles within the organization.

From these four elements Crozier develops his model of a vicious cycle of bureaucracy (Crozier refers to the similar observations Gouldner made about the gypsum mine): the meticulous regulation, the centralization of decision-making, the stratification into isolated units and the informal power struggles which mutually reinforce each other. Crozier concluded that bureaucratic organizations are unable to enter into a self-corrective mode and change. Dysfunctionalities therefore remain an integral part of the self-reinforcing mode. Hence, it takes a crisis to make these organizations adapt.

The Bureaucratic Phenomenon was an instant success and cemented Crozier's reputation in both theory and empirical research as someone who wanted to address what he saw as key issues in French society – in particular, its inability to deal with change. In the 1960s, Crozier founded the *Centre de Sociologie des Organisations* (CSO), which still provides an outstanding home for the sociology of organizations in France. Initially, Crozier brought together a group of young researchers (Erhard Friedberg, Pierre Gremion, Catherine Gremion, Jean-Claude Thoenig, Catherine Balle) and developed a research programme that dealt with French public administration and the difficulties of organizational change.

Crozier departs from what he considers to be the overly harmonious functionalist view of the Columbia School (Crozier and Friedberg, 1976). Instead, he focuses on power relations that unfold at all levels of hierarchy as uncertainties are to be found in many places. He rejects the view that individuals, no matter how far down in the hierarchy they are placed, are determined by their positions and regards all organizational members as partly bound, partly autonomous agents that pursue their interests in a strategic manner, albeit only boundedly rational (a concept from the Carnegie school).

Already in *The Bureaucratic Phenomenon*, Crozier had laid out the ingredients of his notion of organizations as ensembles of games with different rules and rationalities that he later elaborated together with Erhard Friedberg (1980). Crozier was a bridge between European and North American theorizing about organizations, although his reception in North America was somewhat limited to his insights about bureaucracy. His ideas about uncertainty and power inspired the strategic contingencies theory of power (Hickson, Hinings, Schneck, Pennings and Lee, 1971); the game perspective and the micropolitical insights remained largely neglected. On the European continent, however, this work became very influential sparking political and micropolitical approaches that provided a counterfoil to the heavily quantitative contingency studies with their structurally deterministic touch.

Crozier was critical of the developments in organization research at his time. For him, the bureaucracy studies had placed too much emphasis on processes within organizations instead of making the organization itself the level of analysis. Equally, he took issue with the quantitative, deductive turn organization research was taking. He criticized the determinism he saw as inherent in these studies, the a-cultural view, and the overemphasis on structure as the only mediating link between environment and organization, something too simplistic for complex organizations. He concludes, 'this paradigm has led to more and more formalistic studies and less and less meaningful results' (Crozier, 1974, in Pugh, 1985: 108).

The Carnegie School of Decision Making: Rationality Revisited

Let us briefly recapitulate the 'state of affairs' in organization research after World War II: the human relations movement had challenged the machine model of classical management, stressing emotionality and the non-rational character of many organizational activities. Rationality and formal organization were also coming under attack from the scholars of bureaucracy. There was a turn away from the rationalistic imagery of formal organizations, but one that was again quite different.

The key protagonists of the early developments of the decision-making school are Herbert Simon (1916–2001), James March (1928–) and Richard Cyert (1921–1998), all at the Carnegie Institute of Technology. Since they intensively collaborated and co-authored central publications, we discuss their work together. Herbert Simon was a giant of the social sciences. Born to German immigrants in the USA, he received his PhD in political sciences at the University of Chicago. From 1949 until his death, he was on the faculty at Carnegie Mellon University. In 1978, he received the Nobel Prize in economics. His classic, *Administrative Behavior*, was based on his doctoral dissertation and was first published in 1947. Apart from laying the foundations for theorizing about organizational decision-making which is our interest here, Simon made outstanding contributions to computer science and artificial intelligence, receiving the Turing Award in 1975 and the von Neumann Theory Prize in 1988.

James March is professor emeritus at Stanford University, where he began working in 1970. He was also trained as a political scientist with his doctorate from Yale. Between 1953 and 1964, he was at Carnegie together with Simon and Cyert. Richard Cyert (1921–1998) was trained as an economist and statistician with a PhD from Columbia University. He went to Carnegie in 1948 and in 1972 became president of the university serving until his retirement in 1990. Apart from his work on the behavioral theory of the firm, he made significant contributions to Bayesian statistics and experimental economics. For Simon, March and Cyert and their collaborators, the distinctions between macro and micro organization theory or disciplinary boundaries between sociology, psychology, political science and economics were hardly relevant. The ideas they developed were truly interdisciplinary aimed at building a general theory of organizational decision-making.

The significance of the Carnegie school lies in its emphasis on decision-making as the heart of organizations, conceptualizing organizations as decision-making systems. The classic texts are Simon's *Administrative Behavior* (1947; further editions of the book were produced in 1957, 1976 and 1997), March and Simon's *Organizations* (1958) and Cyert and March's *A Behavioral Theory of the Firm* published in 1963 but developed around a number of papers in the 1950s (Augier, 2013).

Simon's work is particularly foundational, as it lays out concepts important in all subsequent Carnegie work, as well as in all thinking about organizational decision-making. He starts with a critique of the principles of management formulated by the classical writers. He notes that they are actually like proverbs that sound very convincing but do not add up to a consistent body of insights, and, if put side by side, often contradict each other. He concludes that they 'are really only criteria for describing and diagnosing administrative situations' (1957: 36), rather than instructions or principles on how to make decisions. For him, organizations are not the result of structural principles but of individual assessments and decisions, however, not in the sense of the non-rational, emotional, and sentiment-driven view of actors that the human relations movement had painted. Human agency (the approach refers to 'behaviour' to distinguish this approach from structuralist views) is purposive, intendedly rational, albeit only boundedly so; hence, organizations are systems of boundedly rational decisions. In fact, bounded rationality is the reason why organizations exist, an insight that became central for transaction cost analysis (Williamson gained his PhD in 1963 at Carnegie): 'Organization will have structure ... insofar as there are boundaries of rationality ... If there were not boundaries of rationality, or if the boundaries varied in a rapid and unpredictable manner, there could be no stable organization structure' (March and Simon, 1958: 170).

A first step offered insights into why people decide to participate and contribute to organizations. Chester Barnard (who wrote a foreword to the first edition of *Administrative Behavior*) influenced Simon. Barnard had emphasized organizations as system of activities that are coordinated to achieve a particular goal. For Barnard, the existence of shared objectives among the members was a given, and the role of executives was to inoculate this organizational purpose as a belief among members. Simon and the Carnegie school gave up the fiction of organizational goals shared by all members; instead, they accepted the multifacetedness of individual goals and stressed that no organization can exist without its members' belief that they are receiving an adequate return for their participation and contributions. They developed and specified the inducement-contribution balance approach and made it a central component of their decision-making theory.

A key idea in *Administrative Behavior*, which became central to Carnegie theorizing is *bounded rationality* although Simon (1947) initially spoke of 'limits to rationality'. Simon was taking on, directly, the idea of economic man where complete rationality and optimization reigned supreme. Instead, Simon argued that the rationality of decision-makers is limited by a number of things, including cognitive limitations, the nature of the decision problem (programmed or non-programmed), and the time available to make a decision. Because of these limitations, optimal decisions are not possible and *satisficing* takes place; the decision solution is one that is satisfactory.

In their elaborations, March and Simon (1958) made the viewpoints of organizational members central; their rationality is tied to their definitions of the situation which is based on their assumptions about the future, their knowledge about alternatives, ordering principles as well as their preferences. With this, they anticipated the interpretative approaches that started to take shape a decade later. They also highlight that decision-makers are subjected to a cognitive attention bias in that they 'can attend to only a limited number of things at a time ... Rational behavior involves substituting for the complex reality a model of reality that is sufficiently simple to be handled by problem-solving processes' (March and Simon, 1958: 151).

However, not all activities in organizations are decision-making. Routinized performance programmes significantly reduce complexity as they use hardly any cognitive capacities and absorb insecurity. Standard operating procedures make up a major part of what is going on in organizations. This is where organizational structure comes in. March and Simon (1958: 170) distinguish different layers of rules and structure:

> An organization is confronted with a problem like that of Archimedes: in order for an organization to behave adaptively, it needs some stable regulations and procedures that it can employ in carrying out its adaptive practices. Thus, at any given time an organization's programs for performing its tasks are part of its structure, but the least stable part. Slightly more stable are the switching rules that determine when it will apply one program, and when another. Still more stable are the procedures it uses for developing, elaborating, instituting, and revising programs.

They distinguish between 'ordinary' decision-making, the choice between existing programs, and organizational learning, changes in the repertoire of programmes.

All of this work is densely packed with theorizing, concepts and arguments covering many topics, culminating in Cyert and March's *A Behavioral Theory of the Firm* (1963; see Gavetti et al., 2012 for an excellent overview). An important part of their argument was that firms are not monolithic but made up of a variety of units with their own interests, values and motivations. Organizational goals are the outcome of negotiations and represent the goals of the dominant coalition at the time. Hence, organizational goals are shifting as coalitions change. As a consequence, multiple goals that are not in harmony with each other coexist. Quasi-solutions such as local rationalities or sequential attention to goals bring a temporary settlement of conflicts arising from diverse sets of goals. Hence, there are not only cognitive restrictions to rationality but also political ones. Later such ideas were extended into organizations as 'organized anarchies' and the 'garbage can model of organizational choice' (Cohen, March, and Olsen, 1972).

The Carnegie school inspired a number of ongoing research programmes, in particular, organizational learning, organizational capabilities and routines. In the late 1960s, before going to Stanford, March spent a year in Scandinavia beginning his collaboration with Johan Olsen with whom March introduced the distinction between the logic of consequentiality and the logic of appropriateness and rediscovered institutions (March and Olson, 1989). SCANCOR was founded – the Scandinavian Consortium for Organizational Research – which heavily influenced North European Organization Analysis (Svejenova, Croidieu and Meyer, 2013). March was 'responsible' for the different twist that institutional theory has always had in Continental Europe!

Conclusions

The 1950s marked both the beginnings and the flowering of the sociological study of organizations. Sociology departments were central players and courses in the sociology of organizations were offered, although the study of organizations was an interdisciplinary endeavour. The Academy of Management was founded in 1936, the British Sociological Association set up an Industrial Sociology group in 1955 and the International Sociological Association followed suit by establishing an Industrial Sociology Research Committee in 1959. The early 1960s saw the establishment of the Centre de Sociologie des Organizations by Crozier. Also the business schools were gaining relevance. In the USA, the Ford Foundation played an important role.

At the end of the 1950s and in the early 1960s, the rationality and efficiency of formal bureaucratic structures had been compromised; dysfunctions, informal structures and bounded rationality were established concepts. The one-best-way idea was dead. Although the centre of attention and the level of analysis were no longer society and its development, but the organization itself, organizations were still seen as cultural 'plants' embedded in a socio-historical context. Interest in power and politics had arisen in the studies of Gouldner, Selznick, Blau, Crozier, and Cyert and March; the legal-rational form of authority had lost its own legitimacy.

Methodologically, the distinctive approach of these studies of bureaucracy was the case study. And for the Carnegie school, it was utilizing those case studies and general theoretical insights to produce codified theory. However, by the end of the 1950s, more quantitative, statistically oriented analyses were gaining in currency especially in North America. As the 1960s dawned, the beginnings of more formalized comparative analysis of organizations began.

5 Comparative Management: No One Best Way

Section 3 dealt with the ideas of classical management scholars whose aim was to reflect on their own experiences within organizations and produce ideas and concepts that would make organizations more efficient and effective. Each of these thinkers was searching for key elements (the necessary and sufficient conditions) that were universal. These approaches had become known as the search for the one best way. Similarly, within the sociology of organizations, the theory of bureaucracy had been regarded as *the* key and unitary way of thinking about organizations.

This quest for the one best way was increasingly viewed as futile during the 1950s and 1960s, when academic research started to subject these ideas to empirical analyses and to compare organizations in order to study both similarities and differences among them. The emphasis became one of contextualizing and explaining similarities and differences, suggesting that there are multiple types of organizations and multiple best ways.

Theorizing about organizations in the 1950s and 1960s was based on three main premises. First, organizations are open social systems that are connected to their environment. Second, there is no universal model of bureaucratic organization and no one best way, but a plurality of organizational forms. Third, this plurality is to be detected in systematic, comparative mostly large-scale empirical studies. These premises led to comparative management theory and, from it, contingency theory, summarized by Van de Ven et al. (2013) as 'an analytical description of organizations; the external circumstances that produce particular organizational designs; and the idea that there is an appropriate linkage between the external, the internal, and performance'. In this section, we examine these premises.

The First Premise: Organizations as Open Systems

Organizations were increasingly conceived as open systems, and researchers started to apply systems theory to organizational study. Although general systems theory was not concerned with organizations per se, writers such as von Bertalanffy (1956) argued that all systems have certain characteristics regardless of whether they are biological, ecological, social or organizational. Systems can vary from simple to complex depending on the kinds of elements (in organizations such elements can be 'activities', 'processes' or 'structures') and the degree of their interdependence (Wiener,1956). Systems ideas began to resonate in organizational research. The view of resources as inputs coming from the environment, being throughput in the organizations to form products and services which are outputs back into the environment was an important part of such conceptualization (Boulding, 1956). In particular, an open systems perspective emphasizing that an organization is itself a system, which is embedded in and interacts with its context or environment, fell on fertile ground. Ideas of survival as an objective for organizations, notions of equilibrium as the desired state, questions of uncertainty and dynamics of environmental change as well as boundary spanning between elements inside the system and between system and the environment entered organizational research.

Talcott Parsons's (1951) structural-functionalist open systems approach was one of the most influential sociological theories in North America after World War II. He conceptualized social systems as made up of subsystems embedded within wider social systems forming nested, embedded and interlocking systems (Parsons, 1956a, 1956b). Subsystems *within* organizations – such as departments, work groups – were essentially the units or building blocks of organizations; systems within which an organization is embedded were local communities and the wider society with its institutional framework. Congruent with the sociological *Zeitgeist* at the time, Parsons's theorizing assumed that there are basic functional requirements (goal achievement, adaptation, integration and latency) that any system must fulfil to survive.

Classical management theorists had often thought in a functionalist way of organizations as systems. Fayol, for example, wrote of generic activities that all organizations have to undertake. Barnard was another early proponent of the idea that organizations should be seen as systems of activities: 'A cooperative system is incessantly dynamic, a process of continual readjustment to physical, biological and social environments as a whole' (Barnard, 1938: 23). As a result of the massive rebuilding of states in Europe after World War II, there was an emerging interest in understanding large-scale organizations that were appearing across all societal sectors. In Germany, it was especially Niklas Luhmann who advanced systems thinking in sociology and organization theory. His early systems approach focused on organizations and their structures as ways to reduce complexity (1964). Twenty years later, his 'autopoietic turn' would move away again from open systems models and establish the operational closure of organizations as self-referential, autopoietic social systems (Luhmann, 1984).

We examine the Tavistock Institute's ideas of organization as a socio-technical system; Katz and Kahn's social psychological view of organizations and, finally, the work of James Thompson.

The Tavistock Institute and Organizations as Socio-technical Systems

An empirically grounded approach to the study of organizations as open systems came from the Tavistock Institute of Human Relations in the UK during the 1950s (the Tavistock Institute recently celebrated its 70th anniversary as did its journal, *Human Relations*). Studying technical change in a British coal mine, Trist and Bamforth (1951) saw organizations as composed of social and technical elements that need to be attended to and, as they are interdependent, aligned – organizations are 'socio-technical systems'. They were criticizing the effect of the Tayloristic work organization that had been introduced in the coal mine because it ignored social aspects and rather than increasing performance, it undermined the organization's performance. A later study of an Indian textile mill (Rice, 1958) elaborated this idea, showing how the socio-technical system at the supervisory level was nested within other organizational systems of control and communication. For Rice, a key element of any supervisory role is managing the 'boundary conditions' between the technical and social systems of an organization because of their interdependence.

Emery and Trist (1965) continued to focus on the relationship between the social and the technical, portraying an organization as taking resources from its environment, converting those resources internally through the socio-technical system into outputs that were then exported back into the environment. They saw these relationships between internal and external systems as dynamic with continual interchange taking place across organizational boundaries. They argued that environments were becoming more turbulent with increasing interconnection between actors in the organization and the environment. The organization, conceptualized as a system, interacts with the environment, also conceptualized as a system.

For the Tavistock researchers, new organizational design principles were required. Traditionally, they argued, through bureaucracy the aim of management was to reduce variety and standardize functions. Instead, they suggested that there should be two principles at play, namely, *redundancy of functions* and *quality of working life*. The systemic nature of organizations in turbulent environments meant having sub-units and individuals with wider ranges of activities and with values that improved the quality of working life through autonomous working groups and collaboration, emphasizing democracy at work. Much of the Tavistock Institute's work in the 1960s and early 1970s is summarized in Emery and Thorsrud (1976).

While the researchers at the Tavistock Institute were concerned with utilizing systems theory to improve both organizational design and organizational democracy in existing organizations, the development of organizational systems theory in North America was more abstract and less empirically based.

Daniel Katz, Robert Kahn and Organizations as 'Flagrantly Open Systems

Robert (Bob) Kahn (1918–) and Daniel Katz (1903–1998) spent most of their academic careers at the University of Michigan. They were associated with the Institute for Social Research (IRS) founded by Rensis Likert. The publication of *The Social Psychology of Organizations* in 1966 is celebrated by ISR as milestone in its history. The website states, 'Robert Kahn's and Daniel Katz's pioneering book influenced the field of organizational research by applying a framework of open system theory – the assumption that an organization continuously interacts with its environment – to research on leadership, role behavior, and organizational effectiveness' (http://home.isr.umich.edu/about/history/timeline/).

Katz and Kahn describe organizations as 'flagrantly open systems' (1966: 17). They emphasize that systems theory 'is basically concerned with problems of relationships, of structure, and of interdependence rather than with the constant attributes of objects' (1966: 22). Katz and Kahn build on sociological theories, especially Parsons's structural-functionalism, as well as psychological thinking from the work of Lewin, Likert and Trist. In Katz and Kahn's framework, organizations are composed of five interrelated subsystems that meet the organization's functional needs: production (concerned with throughput), supportive (dealing with obtaining input and releasing output), maintenance (ensuring conformance of people with their roles), adaptive (dealing with environmental and organizational change) and managerial. Management is about the direction, control and coordination of the other four subsystems and is therefore the apex of an organization.

The Social Psychology of Organizations is an incredibly rich book utilizing concepts such as negative entropy, equifinality, feedback loops and homeostasis and dealing with issues such as power and authority structures, leadership, organizations as role systems, ideology, communication and many more, but our purpose is to briefly restate the core principles with which they were working. Katz and Kahn's approach was *open* systems theory. They saw the systems view as a way of bringing a dynamism into the analysis of organizations that they found missing from organizational theory at the time. They emphasized the importance of the environment in which an organization is located. Thus, organization theory was moved away from prioritizing internal operation. This is, of course, now a taken-for-granted element in studying organizations, and it is difficult to imagine that there was a time in our theorizing when the environmental context of organizations was not seen as crucial.

James D. Thompson and the Paradox of Administration

A seminal contribution to an open systems theory of organization was Thompson's *Organizations in Action* (1967). James D. Thompson (1920–1973) received his PhD in sociology from the University of North Carolina. His first position, in 1954, was in the School of Business and Public Administration at Cornell University. He helped found, and was the first editor of, *Administrative Science Quarterly* in 1956. He later directed the Administrative Science Center, University of Pittsburgh, and then taught in the Sociology Department at Vanderbilt. He died at a relatively young age from cancer.

Organizations in Action is a true classic of organization theory with more than 25,000 citations on Google Scholar. Thompson was attempting to systematize much of the discussion of the previous two decades and to unify existing approaches to understanding organizations by firmly stating that they are open systems, but recognizing their attempts to close themselves to reduce uncertainty: 'we will conceive of complex organizations as open systems, hence indeterminate and faced with uncertainty, but at the same time as subject to criteria of rationality and hence needing determinateness and certainty' (Thompson, 1967: 10). The idea of uncertainty is central for Thompson, and the environment is the key source of uncertainty. Consequently, 'Uncertainty appears as the fundamental problem for complex organizations, and coping with uncertainty, as the essence of the administrative process' (1967: 159). The rational tendencies of organizations mean that they try to protect key elements, such as their 'technological core', from uncertainty. Thompson highlighted that this structural and procedural simultaneousness of openness and closure constitutes a fundamental duality that organizations need to address: 'the paradox of administration' which implies 'the dual searches for certainty and flexibility' (Thompson, 1967: 150).

To take this further, Thompson uses Parsons's (1960) distinctions among three levels of responsibility and control: technical, institutional and managerial. The technical level deals with turning inputs into outputs – the products and services of an organization. This is the particular level where attempts are undertaken to close the system and buffer workings from uncertainty in a rational way. The institutional level is where an organization is part of a wider social system, defining an organization as an open system. Here, uncertainty is greatest as 'the organization deals largely with elements of the environment over which it has no formal authority or control. Instead, it is subjected to generalized norms, ranging from formally codified law to informal standards of good practice, to public authority, or to elements expressing the public interest' (Thompson, 1967: 12). The managerial level services and controls the technical level. It is where inputs are procured and production, control, and human resource systems are designed and managed. The managerial level is also expected to mediate between the other two levels.

Essentially Thompson was concerned with the appropriateness of organization design strategies under conditions of the 'administrative paradox'. As a systems theorist, he saw specifying the ways in which different systems and activities were linked as critical. In particular, he emphasized how technologies are associated with different forms of interdependence between sub-units. His framework has three technologies – *mediating, long-linked* and *intensive* – which have distinctive patterns of interdependences – *pooled, sequential* and *reciprocal* – and use different structural and systemic elements for dealing with uncertainty: a mediating technology is where tasks take place through *pooled interdependence*. In pooled interdependence, organizations form specialized sub-units which are not directly linked but each contributes to the overall whole. Conglomerates or highly diversified corporations are examples. Long-linked technology occurs where there is *sequential interdependence*: one task or activity leads directly to another as in assembly lines. Activities are directly connected in a workflow, horizontally, vertically or both; outputs from one unit are inputs for the next. Sequential interdependence requires a planning system and controls that monitor activities. In an intensive technology, tasks are carried out with *reciprocal interdependence*. It is intensive because the connections between sub-units, tasks, activities and systems are two-way, with inputs and outputs moving backwards and forwards between the units. These are team-based organizations with mutual adjustment as a main mechanism.

Much of classical management theory had been about managing relationships within an organization often regarding the organization as a closed system. Thompson's work is important not only for opening up the organizational system by focusing on the uncertainty and complexity of the environment but also for emphasizing the necessity for organizations to come to terms with the dual requirements of flexibility *and* predictability, of their essential openness *and* the need to buffer their technical core from uncertainty. *Organizations in Action* is a detailed and complex book with many propositions about rationality, uncertainty, complexity and organizational design. Its approach and concepts continue to resonate with today's issues.

The Second Premise: Beyond Bureaucracy as a Unitary Form

The works of Merton, Blau, Gouldner, Selznick and Crozier were classic case studies of the internal workings of bureaucracy and its dysfunctions, emphasizing informal structure, interests and power. Their purpose was to show that Weber's analysis of the formal, intended characteristics of bureaucracy missed unintended consequences which disrupt organizational goals and activities. In addition, researchers started to show that bureaucratic functioning is influenced by behavioural factors that Weber failed to consider such as non-Western cultures (Berger, 1956; Shor, 1960) or the non-bureaucratic identification of organizational members (Brown, 1954; Gouldner, 1957). These studies led to new developments in theorizing bureaucracy.

One development was to create new analytical types, classifying organizations into typologies and taxonomies. Such classifications aimed at discovering varieties of organizational genotypes as specific configurations of components or *Gestalt*. Bureaucracy studies noted that there are different kinds of bureaucracy (Gerth, 1952; Gouldner, 1957; Stinchcombe, 1959; Presthus, 1961). Other researchers formed typologies based on technology (Thompson, 1967; Perrow, 1972) or management systems (Burns and Stalker, 1961). Blau and Scott (1962) created a typology based on the 'cui bono' question distinguishing between mutual benefit associations (members as prime beneficiaries), business concerns (benefitting owners), service organizations (the clients) and commonwealth organizations (the public). Etzioni (1961) distinguishes three kinds of power (coercive, remunerative and normative) and three kinds of involvement of organizational members (alienative, calculative and moral) as a base for his typology. From the combination of power and involvement, nine possible types of compliance structure are generated. Etzioni calls three of them congruent types, meaning that forms of power and of involvement are aligned: coercive organizations (coercive power and alienative involvement, e.g. in prisons), utilitarian organizations (remunerative power and calculative commitment, e.g. business organizations) and normative organizations (normative power and moral involvement, e.g. church organizations). Incongruent types are those where the two aspects are misaligned. For Etzioni, congruent organizations are more effective than non-congruent ones.

Another development was to challenge the unitary nature of the concept of bureaucracy. As (US) sociologists wrestled throughout the 1950s with the concept of bureaucracy empirically, it became apparent that essentially bureaucracy had been regarded as unidimensional, as one 'block', so all the bureaucratic elements could be found together and would differ in synch (as we have noted previously, this actually misses the Weberian idea of an ideal type). In the 1950s and into the 1960s, more and more calls were voiced for a general theory of organizations, one that was based on examining and discovering general tendencies of how the various elements of bureaucracy came together in different real-life organizations. Udy (1959) and Stinchcombe (1959) were at the start of this process. Udy suggested a possible lack of correlation between the Weberian elements of bureaucracy and, indeed, showed that there was no association between what he called 'bureaucratic' and 'rational' elements. Stinchcombe's findings were similar, demonstrating that some elements (stable jurisdictions, official duties and authority) are characteristic of a generic rational approach to organizing and that continuity of tasks, hierarchy and the use of files are specific components of a bureaucracy. Both Udy and Stinchcombe showed empirically that the elements of bureaucratic structure did not necessarily correlate and, hence, did not describe an inherently coherent set. This work was highly influential, beginning the process of utilizing bureaucracy not as *the* key way of thinking of organizations but as a way of generating a more comprehensive theory of organizations. Indeed, Presthus (1959: 25) called for 'an explicit synthesis between conceptual theory and empirical field research' to develop such a theory. In subsequent research, bureaucracy was still used as a starting point. The elements specified by Weber were operationalized and the relationships between them examined. A new assumption was that they could vary in a number of ways across organizations.

This approach utilized Weberian insights in a purely structural way, moving away from notions of dynamics, power and dysfunctions. Organizations were conceptualized as primarily structural phenomena, and large-scale, bureaucratic organizations still dominated and set research agendas. In the 1960s, this agenda was particularly worked out through the studies of Richard (Dick) Hall, Jerald (Jerry) Hage and Michael (Mike) Aiken (Hall, 1963a, 1963b, 1967, 1968; Hall and Tittle, 1966; Hage and Aiken, 1967a, 1967b, 1969; Hall, Haas and Johnson, 1967). The title of the first paper published by Hall in 1963 in *Administrative Science Quarterly* summarizes what this agenda was about: 'The concept of bureaucracy: An empirical assessment'. These studies conceptualized bureaucracy as a set of structural dimensions that can be systematically measured. Hall (1963a), for example, worked with seven dimensions – hierarchy of authority, division of labour, technical competence, work procedures, positional rules, prescribed authority and differential rewards – and found that an emphasis on technical qualifications was negatively correlated with the other elements. This led to future work (Hall, 1968) on the relationship between bureaucratic elements and professional ones, essentially a long and ongoing debate on the opposition between professional and bureaucratic organizations. Drawing on the insights of Durkheim as well as Weber, Hage and Aiken (1967a) examined the way in which complexity, centralization and formalization related to innovation in a medical setting, showing that high complexity, decentralization and low formalization are characteristics of an innovative organization.

The emphasis in this work was to establish organizational differences, to show that bureaucracy was just one organizational form among others. The elements put forward by Weber as characteristic of a bureaucracy were transformed into the more general organizational constructs of specialization, centralization, standardization, formalization and complexity, operationalized as variables and, then, showing empirically how these elements are interrelated. Formal bureaucracies (high specialization, standardization, formalization and complexity together with centralization) can be distinguished from more simple structures (Mintzberg, 1979) with the opposite structural features to those of the bureaucracy. Breaking up bureaucracy into a set of dimensions opened organizational research for the possibility of many other combinations of these dimensions. For example, Pugh, Hickson Hinings and Turner (1969b) distinguished between full bureaucracies and workflow bureaucracies, the former being where specialized roles, rules and procedures covered all organizational activities and the latter where it was the production processes only that were subject to bureaucratic elements.

Apart from the idea of turning the elements of Weber's ideal type into variables, there were two other important impulses that came from this line of research. One was to move away from single case studies to comparative studies; comparative meant large-scale. The studies all had large (for the times!) samples of organizations to examine how far the elements of bureaucracy cohered with statistical methods to analyse these data sets. The second important consequence was to set off the interest in understanding why these differences occurred and what caused them. In particular, this work suggested two features that affect the structural form of an organization. One was size (Hall, Haase and Johnson, 1967); the other was technology (Udy, 1959; Hage and Aiken, 1969; Perrow, 1970); open systems models added a third: the environment.

The Third Premise: The Systematic Study of Organizational Differences

Several academic works exemplify the turn in the late 1950s and 1960s to examining multiple organizations systematically and the initial development of contingency theory, most prominently, Woodward (1958, 1965); Burns and Stalker (1961); Lawrence and Lorsch (1967a, 1967b), as well as the so-called Aston Group (Pugh et al, 1963; Pugh, Hickson, Hinings and Turner, 1968; Pugh, Hickson and Hinings, 1969a; Pugh et al., 1969b). These seminal works are dealt with next.

Joan Woodward and the Impact of Technology

Joan Woodward (1916–1971) was an early pioneer in systematically examining the claims of the practitioner-scholars. Her initial work was published in the 1950s (Woodward, 1958) – earlier than her colleagues and leading the way. There are some very interesting elements to her career. First, she was part of a post–World War II policy interest in the role of organizations in industrial reconstruction. As such, the British Government through the Department of Scientific and Industrial Research funded her research. It was a time when organizations were seen as important to industrial policy and when the Marshall Plan was funding industrial social research (Klein, 2010). Second, her work was carried out at the South East Essex College of Technology, a non-university institution. There were no university-based business schools in the UK in the 1950s; those business schools that did exist were located in technical colleges such as South East Essex or the Birmingham College of Advanced Technology that hosted the Aston Group. Third, she moved from that 'lowly' college to the prestigious Imperial College of Science and Technology, one of the leading science and engineering schools in the world. Joan Woodward was located in Production Engineering as there was no business school. In 1969, she was appointed professor of Industrial Sociology and director of the Industrial Sociology Unit, only the second woman to be appointed to a chaired professorship at Imperial College. Unfortunately, Joan Woodward died in 1971 at the age of 54 of breast cancer. Her legacy lives on in her pioneering scholarship and in the biannual Joan Woodward Memorial Lecture and the Joan Woodward Prize at Imperial College Business School. Much more about her life and career can be found in the tribute to her, *Technology and Organization: Essays in Honour of Joan Woodward* (Phillips, Sewell and Griffiths, 2010).

Her research used a sample of 100 organizations in South East Essex (where Ford Motors was the dominant employer), a sample size that was highly unusual for the 1950s. Her work was a critique of the one best way philosophy that dominated organizational research at the time. She herself commented later (Woodward, 1965), 'the danger lies in the tendency to teach the principles of administration as though they were scientific laws, when they are really little more than administrative expedients found to work well in certain circumstances but never tested in any systematic way' (quoted in Pugh and Hickson, 2007: 13).

Woodward's first innovation was to clearly specify the elements that classical management theorists talked about when referring to organizational structure. Thus, she dealt with highly specific organizational features, including the number of levels in the hierarchy, spans of control of supervisors, the degree of definition of roles, the division of specialist functions and the extent of written communication (Woodward, 1958). The sample of organizations that she studied showed wide variation on all of these measures, indicating that there were no generalizable principles. This led her to ask why such differences occurred. In examining a variety of potential explanations such as differences in size, type of industry or historical development, Woodward and her team made the following observation: 'When, however, the forms were grouped according to similarity of objectives and techniques of production, and classified in order of the technical complexity of their production systems, each production system was found to be associated with a characteristic pattern of organization' (Woodward, 1958, reprinted in Pugh, 1985: 52). They came to the conclusion that technology was a major influence on organizational structure: not the only one, but a very important one. What she argued was that the objectives of an organization and the markets that it serves determine the kind of technology employed, which in turn has a key impact on the structure of the organization.

Out of this initial research came the central idea about the role of technology and an entire research programme (Woodward, 1965; 1970). Woodward's notion of technology was to think of it as being embedded in production systems that differed in their degree of technical complexity. It is important to remember that the context for her research was manufacturing industry – after all, at that time, the UK was a country that mainly produced manufactured goods. Woodward (1958) introduced three broad categories of technical production systems: unit and small batch production, large batch and mass production and finally process production. Each of these was subdivided further, e.g. the second into production of large batches, production of large batches on an assembly line and mass production.

Woodward also recognized that in dealing with organization structures and technology, she was examining systems of management control (Woodward, 1965). She and her colleagues used a two-dimensional classification framework with one dimension being 'personal/impersonal' and the other 'fragmented/unified'. For Woodward, appropriateness of different systems of management control, e.g. personal/unified or impersonal/fragmented, was directly related to the technology used. Thus, with unit and small batch production, there would be unitary and mainly personal controls, whereas process production involves unitary and impersonal administrative and mechanical controls.

Joan Woodward's work was pioneering in many ways. She set out a fresh way of thinking about organizations, their control systems and technology, emphasizing that the quest for a one best way had to be replaced by a systematic search for differences. She emphasized that 'The criterion of the appropriateness of an organizational structure must be the extent to which it furthers the objectives of the firm, not as management teaching sometimes suggest, the degree to which it conforms to a prescribed pattern. There can be no one best way of organizing a business' (Woodward, 1958, reprinted in Pugh, 1985: 57). She examined these ideas through large-scale empirical investigation that was based in a deep understanding of the organizations and the contexts in which they operated. As Pugh et al. (1985: 31) put it, 'she forces thinking away from the abstract elaboration of principles of administration to an examination of the constraints placed on organization structure and management practice by differing technologies and their associated control structures.' In addition, she pioneered being a woman in the intensely male world of Imperial College (and organization research more generally) and left a legacy which still lives in the Imperial College Business School.

Tom Burns and the Politics of Innovation and Organizational Change

Around the same time that Woodward was carrying out her initial work in South East Essex, British sociologist Tom Burns (1913–2001) and his initial collaborator, the psychologist George Stalker, were conducting their research for the Scottish Council (Development and Industry) 'to facilitate the entry of Scottish firms with the right resources into electronic development work and, eventually, manufacture' (Burns and Stalker, 1961: 3). When presenting their findings during 1955–1956, Burns was asked by the UK Ministry of Supply to study the electronics industry in England. The central concern of the Scottish and English studies was to examine the difficulties of organizations dealing with rapid technical change and, in particular, the problem of getting researched-based groups engaged with innovation, development and design to work effectively with production and sales.

The Management of Innovation became known for the distinction between two ideal types of management systems: mechanistic and organismic (or organic as this type is now mostly called). Not only did Burns and Stalker make that primary distinction, but they also related it to the idea of internal (task) and external (environment) uncertainty. The mechanistic organization is very similar to the rational bureaucracy as studied by Weber and earlier sociologists of organization, exhibiting clear hierarchy, specialization through a division of labour, detailed and clear rules and procedures, with communication systems based on formal position and authority. It is a programmed, machine-like organization. In contrast, organic organizations have a relative absence of formal control systems and emphasize expertise. They rely on continuous high levels of interactions between units and individuals, and those interactions are based on the ability to assist and a willingness to experiment and adjust.

The lasting legacy of Burns and Stalker has been the distinction between mechanistic and organic management systems (Sine, Mitsuhashi and Kirsch, 2006). In developing this distinction, they stressed the idea of 'appropriate alignment' to the environment in which an organization is located, and to the tasks that it performs. While Woodward had emphasized task complexity, Burns stressed task uncertainty. Electronics organizations in the 1950s were building such things as computers and their components which were highly unstandardized. These were the very early days of computers, 30 years before they became available as personal computers; they were machines that took up very large rooms and turnaround of computations was counted in days not minutes or seconds. In other words, there was a great deal of uncertainty on how to carry out the task. Similarly, the market for electronics, for TVs, computers and hi-fi was just developing. Again that meant a high degree of uncertainty in the organizational environment. Those two uncertainties – task and environmental – required an organic, flexible, highly interactive organization. At the other end of the spectrum is the organization producing a standard product to a known market. For example, an organization producing railway sleepers/ties where every sleeper is like the next one, standard dimensions, holes drilled in the same place, made of wood. The demand for such a product can be easily forecast in terms of the plans for track laying by the main railways. Thus, there is considerable task and environmental certainty which favours a mechanistic organization where everything can be clearly defined – jobs, authority, production procedures, communication systems.

Thus, the mechanistic organization performs well where there are both environmental and task certainty. Stable conditions, where markets and products are either not changing or do so in predictable ways, means that the organization can be programmed to operate in a machine-like manner. The organic organization thrives where there are high levels of environmental and task uncertainty and unpredictability of future developments. It can cope with new and unfamiliar issues in markets and products through adjustment and mutuality. As Donaldson (2001: 37) puts it, Burns and Stalker offer 'an elegant theory that has proved to be compelling for many subsequent scholars' – maybe because their work was reduced to a simplified typology classifying organizations as 'mechanistic' or 'organic'.

Recently, Hinings et al. (2018) argued that at the heart of Tom Burns's work, in particular, was the politics of change rather than organizational structures per se, yet this has not been handed down as part of his legacy. Burns (1961, 1977) conceptualized organizations as composed of three interacting and self-reinforcing social systems at work simultaneously: first, the formal authority system that represents the organization's objectives, technologies and hierarchies; second, the status or career system related to individuals' goals and aspirations; and third, the political system in which individuals and sub-units compete for power. He stresses: 'In fact, members of a corporation are at one and the same time co-operators in a common enterprise and rivals for the material and intangible rewards of successful competition with each other. The hierarchic order of rank and power that prevails in them is at the same time a single control system and a career ladder' (Burns, 1961: 261).

Any attempt at organizational change affects all three systems; hence, Burns is very pessimistic as regards an organization's potential to radically change from one type to another. The career and political systems in particular make it extremely difficult for a mechanistic organization to move towards the organic form. As Pugh and Hickson (2007: 33) point out, Burns and Stalker carefully demonstrated this difficulty of organizational change: 'The almost complete failure of the traditional Scottish firms to absorb electronics research and development engineers into their organizations led Burns to doubt whether a mechanistic firm can consciously change into an organismic one.' Indeed, mechanistic organizations become 'pathological' when confronted with change:

The ideology of formal bureaucracy seemed so deeply ingrained in industrial management that the common reaction to unfamiliar and novel conditions was to redefine, in more precise and rigorous terms, the roles and working relationships obtaining within management, along orthodox lines of organization charts and organization manuals. The formal structure was reinforced, not adapted. In these concerns the effort to make the orthodox bureaucratic system work produced what can best be described as pathological forms of the mechanistic system. (Burns, 1963, reprinted in Pugh, 1985: 47)

Burns and Stalker (1961) had distinguished three such pathologies that, although the measures are explicitly taken to change the organization, actually prevent adaptation and perpetuate mechanistic structures. The first, which Burns called the 'ambiguous figure' system is very similar to the vicious circle that Crozier (1964) and Gouldner (1954a) had described. The second, the 'mechanistic jungle' describes how, in order to solve new types of problems, novel organizational functions and departments are established whose continued existence actually depends on the perpetuation of these problems. Third, there is the development of the 'committee system' that entangles the participants in loyalty conflicts.

The Management of Innovation became famous for its two ideal types. However, the underlying *Leitmotif* of the book is the difficulty of change with an emphasis on power, politics and status, yet this was not what was taken up in the 1960s, nor what made it into the typical textbook legacy that continues to this day. This interest in power and politics, however, made Burns (especially Burns, 1961) an important source for the micro-political approach (Crozier and Friedberg, 1980; Küpper and Ortmann, 1988) that became very influential in Continental European organization research in the 1970s and 1980s (Hinings et al., 2018).

Paul Lawrence, Jay Lorsch and the Precarious Balance between Differentiation and Integration

It was Paul Lawrence (1922–2011) and Jay Lorsch (1932–) who actually introduced the term 'contingency theory' (1967a, 1967b) and thereby labelled the dominant way of analyzing organizations in the 1960s and 1970s. Akin to Woodward and Burns and Stalker, Lawrence and Lorsch directly challenged the idea that there was one best way of organizing. To study the effect of different environments, the research that produced *Organization and Environment* was carried out in ten firms in three industries – plastics, food and containers. The core argument of the authors was that organizational effectiveness was derived from an adequate 'fit' of the organization's degree of differentiation, and the means of integration and conflict resolution, with the contingent environmental circumstances in which the organization operates.

The research was carried out at the Harvard Business School (HBS) where both authors were/are based. Paul Lawrence was a professor of Organizational Behavior. He started his lifelong academic career at Harvard in 1947 having received his MBA and PhD there. Jay Lorsch continues to be a professor of Human Relations at HBS where he has spent his academic career since receiving his DBA in 1964. Lawrence was 46 and Lorsch ten years younger when *Organization and Environment* was published. Their work was highly recognized and received the Academy of Management's Best Management Book of the Year Award in 1969.

Organization and Environment is distinctly managerial in focus, asking 'What kind of organization structures are required in firms facing different economic and market conditions?' There is immediately a recognition that organizations operate in different contexts that demand varying responses. Their concepts of 'differentiation' and 'integration' became central for the analysis of structures and processes (Donaldson, 2001; Scott and Davis, 2011). Essentially, the elements of management that classical management theorists elaborated – they had either emphasized the division of labour in organizations or the structures and processes for ensuring unity of purpose and direction – are built into these two basic concepts: *differentiation* concerns the allocation of tasks and responsibilities between organizational sub-units/ departments; *integration* is the achievement of coordinated collective effort amongst those differentiated parts.

The idea of differentiation is directly connected to the existence of departments and sub-units within an organization. In particular, three key functions (research and development, production and sales) were studied. Importantly, while differentiated units are based in functions and tasks which are structurally defined, the differences between them are also reflected in and exacerbated by differences in the cognitive and emotional orientations of their members (such as their temporal orientation, interpersonal orientation or goal orientation). For example, there is likely to be substantial structural differentiation between the functions of production and of research and development which is strengthened by a likely long-time horizon and informality in the latter versus a more short-time oriented view dealing with day-to-day problems in a highly formalized way in the former.

Lawrence and Lorsch's main argument is that the extent of differentiation between sub-units is a function of the environment in which they operate and that environment is itself segmented or differentiated. Thus, the sales department deals with a market sub-environment, production or manufacturing with a technical and economic sub-environment, and research and development with a scientific/engineering sub-environment. The key issue is the degree of uncertainty related to each sub-environment. The degree of uncertainty can vary; hence, the greater the diversity between the sub-environments, the greater the need for organizational differentiation. Lawrence and Lorsch found that the firms in the plastics industry dealt with a stable techno-economic environment but a highly uncertain scientific/engineering environment leading to relatively high differentiation. In the container industry, all sub-environments were relatively stable so much less differentiation was required.

It is the extent of differentiation that produces the need for integration. For Lawrence and Lorsch, these two elements of organization design are 'essentially antagonistic'; hence, dealing with them is a central challenge for managers. They are antagonistic because high levels of differentiation, structurally and cognitively, produce departments and groups that have their own distinctive ways of dealing with the particular uncertainties that they face. Because of the cognitive and emotional aspects, they may involve fundamental differences in ways of thinking and behaving. Successful firms develop integrative devices to bring together the differentiated parts of an organization and to deal with conflict resolution. While all firms used traditional methods such as paper systems and hierarchy, the use of other integrative mechanisms varied with the degree of differentiation (and environmental uncertainty) being faced. Thus, while the standard measures were sufficient for a low differentiation container firm, a food firm, with more differentiation, also used temporary cross-functional teams as well as liaison personnel. A plastics organization with even more differentiation had permanent cross-functional teams as well as a whole sub-unit whose task was departmental integration.

It is, then, the relationship amongst the three elements – environmental diversity and uncertainty, differentiation, and integration – that is important for success and high performance. High environmental uncertainty goes hand in hand with high internal differentiation that requires high levels of integration; low levels of integration under such conditions mean poor performance. Low environmental diversity and uncertainty means low differentiation that requires low integration; having more elaborate integrative devices also means poor performance. Poorer performing organizations either had too much or too little integrative effort, and/or the wrong forms of integration. Balance between differentiation and integration was essential. The core theme of *Organization and Environment* – the challenge of resolving 'essentially antagonistic' relationships between central elements of organizational design – has lost nothing of its relevance today (Hinings et al., 2018).

Within the Harvard Business School, Lawrence and Lorsch developed a research programme that built on the relationship amongst uncertainty, differentiation and integration. In particular, they examined how the framework could be used in managerial action (Lawrence and Lorsch, 1969) and studied the relationship between organizational design elements and individual cognition and behaviour (Lorsch and Morse, 1974). Also, their emphasis on integrative devices was foundational to ideas of the matrix organization which became popularized in the 1970s (Davis and Lawrence, 1977).

The Aston Group and the Flowering of Contingency Theory

The work of Woodward, Burns and Stalker and Lawrence and Lorsch was highly influential. According to Google Scholar, Burns and Stalker and Lawrence and Lorsch have been cited more than 14,000 times, and Woodward more than 8,000 times. Together with the work reviewed in Section 4 on bureaucracy, the comparative study of organizational structure was well and truly launched. Indeed from the late 1960s and through the 1970s, there was a steady stream of studies that was summarized under the label introduced by Lawrence and Lorsch, namely, contingency theory.

An important contributor to this research was the Aston Group at the Birmingham College of Advanced Technology which later became the University of Aston. Like Woodward's research, it was funded by the Department of Scientific and Industrial Research with the aim of understanding organizations in their totality and located outside a university for the first five years of its work. The founder of the research centre was Derek Pugh (1930–2015), a social psychologist who had started his career as a researcher in Edinburgh studying absenteeism and turnover. Another key figure who was with the group from its foundation was David Hickson (1931–2016), who had studied restriction of output in work groups. In the 1970s, Hickson was one of the co-founders of EGOS, the European Group for Organization Studies, and the inaugural editor of its journal *Organization Studies*. Other researchers who contributed to the Aston programme are Bob Hinings, John Child and Diana Pheysey.

The Aston Group conducted a series of comparative studies to produce generalizable insights into the relationship between organizational structure and context. The key analytical results of what became known as the 'Aston studies' were published in *Administrative Science Quarterly* in the late 1960s (Pugh et al., 1968; Pugh et al., 1969a; Pugh et al., 1969b). The studies were important for a number of reasons. With the results of extensive fieldwork, they represented a successful attempt to systematize ideas and explanations that had been developed from the study of bureaucracy and of comparative manage-ment. A clear framework of concepts was developed, initially in Pugh et al. (1963), and, importantly, concepts that dealt systematically with both, internal organizational structure and the context in which organizations are located. Then, empirically, cross-sectional data was collected on a random sample of organizations stratified by size and product/service. The sample size of 46 organizations was large for the time, particularly as all data was collected by means of extensive interviews within each organization. A further important step was that psychometric methods and (for the time) advanced statistical methods were used in analysis. Indeed, the project was the first in studying organizations using psychometric scaling, principal components analysis and an analysis of the multivariate prediction of structure from context. At the time, business education increasingly moved from technical colleges to universities in the UK and such statistical methods were regarded as more sophisticated and objective and, hence, scientific.

Organizational structure was conceptualized on the basis of five variables which were derived from Weber's elements of bureaucracy – specialization, standardization, formalization, centralization and configuration. These vari-ables were not binary but continuous from which scores were produced. The context in which an organization operated and within which organizational structure developed was condensed, described in measures of size, technology, ownership and control; origins and history; charter; dependence; and location (which was dropped in the first studies that drew on samples of organizations in close geographical vicinity).

This research showed that there was considerable variation between organi-zations; Pugh et al. (1969a) established a taxonomy of seven (later condensed into four) empirically derived distinctive types of organization. And impor-tantly, by conceptualizing eight elements of context, they were able to show that key predictors of organizational structure and organizational type were size, dependence on other organizations and integrated technology. The programme generated wide-ranging research, summarized in Pugh and Hickson (1976), Pugh and Hinings (1976), Pugh and Payne (1977) and Hickson and McMillan (1981) including social psychological issues and cross-cultural comparisons.

Conclusions

The 1960s and early 1970s marked a time of the blossoming of the sociology of organization and organization theory. Research-based books appeared that aimed at summarizing the field and suggested future research agendas (Mouzelis, 1967; Perrow, 1970, 1972; Kieser and Kubicek, 1978a, 1978b). Other texts appeared that were focused on organizational design and contingency theory (Galbraith, 1973) and readers that collected key articles (Hall, 1972; Kast and Rozenzweig, 1973). The titles of the latter two books, in particular, as collections, indicate what the central concerns of the time were: *The Formal Organization* (Hall) and *Contingency Views of Organization and Management* (Kast and Rosenzweig). The interest in organizations had started by seeing them as part of society, as representation and, at the same time, drivers of fundamental developments in society. Over the years 'society' was translated into 'operational context' to be expressed in concrete, measurable variables. Consequently, on the methodological level, case studies were replaced by large-scale quantitative analyses. A degree of systematization had taken place, and it seemed to clearly point the way for future research. Many followed this research agenda. A decade later, this way of conducting organizational research would fall victim to its own success.

In the early 1970s, the central 'infrastructure' for organization research was in place: in 1971, the American Sociological Association established a division on Occupations and Organizations; the Organization and Management Theory (OMT) Division of the Academy of Management (AoM) was established in 1969; and at this time, most of the members had been trained in sociology departments. Business schools became increasingly popular and took over much of the study of organizations. Organization theory had arrived as an intellectually stimulating and thriving endeavour.

6 Conclusions

We have covered approximately 120 years of thinking about organizations and ways of understanding and managing them. There is broad consensus that the genesis of organization theory is to be found in the rise of the large-scale, complex organization as a result of the Industrial Revolution and the development of factories and mass production. In the late nineteenth and early twentieth centuries, academics and practitioner-scholars analyzed the rise of this new organizational form and pondered how it emerged and could be managed. As the early writers wrestled with these questions, the sociology of organizations and organization theory were born. It was particularly in the post–World War II era that the academic pursuit of organizational analysis flowered, but also that the institutional infrastructure to support these endeavours came into place.

We have used the distinction between the academic understanding of organizations and the practitioner-scholars' interest in managing them as a way of framing the early days of organization theorizing. One stream of the subsequent development of organization theory consisted of academics subjecting the work of scholar-practitioners to more rigorous analysis. From this, the comparative analysis of organizations evolved. Similarly, the sociology of organizations took off in the 1950s as the Weberian concept of bureaucracy came under scrutiny in terms of its internal dynamics and external pressures on its structure. As the academic study of organizations became paramount, the practitioner approach to organizations became institutionalized outside academia in the rise of management consulting; management consulting thus became a subject for study rather than a partner in the analysis of organizations (Kipping and Engwall, 2002; McKenna, 2006).

Of course, there is a 'so what' aspect to producing an Element like this. Why should we be interested in the history of organization theory, particularly when the current situation is very different and itself complex and fragmented? By the beginning of the 1970s, much of the study of organizations was dominated by a structural perspective on organizations characterized by the study of bureaucracy, systems theory and structural contingency theory. For a brief period of time, there seemed to be a substantial degree of paradigm agreement. However, only a few years later new and relatively well-articulated theories had arisen in the United States – most prominently population ecology (Hannan and Freeman, 1977), institutional theory (Meyer and Rowan, 1977) and resource dependence (Pfeffer and Salancik, 1978). Europe was never dominated in the same way by contingency theory; there, ideas of social action and phenomenological approaches had always been influential and becoming more so (e.g. Luhmann, 1968; Silverman, 1970; Child, 1972; Burrell and Morgan, 1979; Clegg and Dunkerley, 1980; Crozier and Friedberg, 1980). What we have seen in the past 45 years is a proliferation of theoretical and conceptual approaches and topics together with a wide variety of methods. The scholarly associations of organization theorists have grown so that in 2017 the OMT Division of the AoM had more than 4,000 members, and EGOS, its European counterpart, counted more than 2,500 members. Both organizations have members from all around the world. In addition to these two, there are the Australian and New Zealand Academy of Management (ANZAM), the Latin-American and European Meeting on Organization Studies (LAEMOS), the European Academy of Management (EURAM) as well as a variety of associations in Asia.

As contingency theory would tell us, scale is related to differentiation, and differentiation has happened with organization theory. Two recent examples demonstrate this. The *SAGE Handbook of Organization Studies* (Clegg, Hardy, Lawrence and Nord, 2006) has chapters on ecology, organizational economics, complexity science, institutions, critical theory, feminist theory, action research, reflexivity, leadership, decision-making, identity, communication, innovation, environmentalism, globalization, emotion, aesthetics, culture, power, networks, change, compassion and rhetoric. Similarly, within one theoretical perspective, the *SAGE Handbook of Organizational Institutionalism* (Greenwood, Oliver, Lawrence and Meyer, 2017) has 33 chapters including topics such as entrepreneurship, inequality, micro-foundations, social movements, networks, meaning, power, identity, emotions, governance, logics, and globalization. Such is the richness and diversity of the field. This contrasts with the first *Handbook of Organizations* (March, 1965) which had nine chapters on specific organizations, e.g. political parties, the military, schools, hospitals and prisons and included applications of organization theory to organizational design, applied organizational change and inter-personal relationships. Organization theory is a strong, diverse field embracing a wide variety of approaches.

So, given the scale, strength and diversity of current organization studies why should we care about 'ancient' history? Recently Hinings et al. (2018) have argued that most of the organizational classics take a holistic approach to understanding organizations. In doing this, these authors show a deep understanding of the organizations studied. As we have moved away from the research monograph and the overall statements of organization theory, this holistic approach has been lost to a large extent. This is particularly true in North America; Europe remains some-what more welcoming to broader perspectives, although this is changing with the increase of paper-based dissertations and habilitations (the high-est qualification level in some European countries) and formal evaluation and ranking systems that favour journal articles for universities in general and business schools in particular. Yet, 'dusty books' continue to offer insights because of their comprehensive concern with the organization as the unit of study, dealing with systems, structure, politics, power, pro-cesses, routine, change, status and careers as a totality.

Hinings et al. (2018) also argue that the inspiration that these historical texts offer to current themes in organizational studies is unfaltering. One example we mentioned in the previous section is Burns and Stalker (1961) who emphasize the political nature of organizational change and the ways in which it is extremely difficult for organizations of one type to move to another type. Interestingly, many of the classic texts that form what we have called the 'understanding organizations' strand are strongly concerned with power, pol-itics, interests and values – issues that have later been claimed absent in organization theory (Clegg and Hardy, 2006).

Apart from the potential enlightenment of specific themes and issues, we believe that the engagement with beginnings holds two important and closely related learnings for contemporary organization theory. One is a concern with the relationship between organizations and society, and the other is a concern with the emergence of new organizational forms.

The early analysts, Marx, Michels and Weber all locate the emergence of organizations within larger societal developments, and they dealt with the mutual impact of large-scale organizations and the state, the distribution of power within society, changing class structures and other institutions of society. All three were concerned with relationships between organizational elites and societal power structures. They elaborated how overarching societal belief systems are an important element in these relationships. Their insights were strongly related to the rise of complex organizations as a new form of coordinating activities, increasingly referred to as bureaucracy. This concern continued in a number of ways as the importance of this new organizational form for society was emphasized more and more, culminating in books in the 1940s, 1950s and 1960s that highlighted the relationship between the large-scale, complex organization and society (Burnham, 1941; Drucker, 1946; Merton et al., 1952; Boulding, 1953; Whyte, 1956; Presthus, 1962). It is also reflected in the approaches of those practitioner-scholars who dealt with the management of these organizations. On the one hand, they recognized the need to have new approaches to, and methods of, management. On the other hand, they saw the importance of this new organizational form for society and believed that through efficient and effective management, society would be improved. But, no matter whether seen from the academic or the scholar-practitioner perspective, organizational theory took off because of the centrality of organizations as *societal* institutions.

Why does this matter? We believe that with the increasing number of organizational concepts and theories and the complexity of their relationships to one another, organizational theorizing often seems to be turning into some kind of navel-gazing preoccupied with its own inventions. As a consequence, the relationship between society and organizations or organizational forms disappears from the radar.

From an organization theory perspective, the organization as a holistic unit of analysis has become secondary. Greenwood, Hinings and Whetten (2014) argued that within institutional theory, the organization per se has become less important as a unit of analysis despite the fact that institutional theory emerged as an alternative theory of why organizations are structured as they are. The early theorists remind us of the centrality of the organization to organization theory. They also remind us of the insights only a comprehensive view can gain. Of course, given the strong differentiation of ideas, approaches and concepts within organization theory, this is a difficult task. We do not mean to promote a search for a unified paradigm, quite the contrary. But we are wondering, where the integrators and boundary spanners are who can bring some of these fragmented elements together to form a bigger picture? How can this be accomplished in a climate in which each and every article is required to bring even more conceptual innovations to the field, and 'speaking to too many literatures' has become a knockout criterion in the publication game?

Taking the relationship of organizations and society seriously includes also a concern with how organizations are managed. The practitioner-scholars attempted to answer this question prescriptively and subsequently found themselves subject to academic analysis which challenged such notions. Integrating management education in higher education and establishing business schools within universities has (rightly, we say) increased the demand for research to adhere to academic standards which, however, entailed that organizational research became more and more detached from the experiences of practitioners. Over the past decade, there has been an increasing debate on the relevance of organizational research – that is, relevance to those whose task it is to manage the organizations we study, in particular through the use of evidence-based management (Rousseau and McCarthy, 2007; Kieser and Leiner, 2009; Reay, Berta and Kohn, 2009). It is not that there is an absence of voices on how contemporary organizations should be managed. However, the proliferation of such voices is mostly due to the rise of management consulting (Kipping and Engwall, 2002; McKenna, 2006) (and many consultants are the graduates of MBA programmes). There is a delicate relationship between academic research and advice that is currently under scrutiny.

It was the appearance and rise of a new kind of organization within a particular societal context that sparked interest both in understanding organizations and in managing them. This is particularly germane as the development of society is ongoing and new forms of organizing continue to emerge. Meyer and Höllerer (2014) make this a central point when they argue that the classic formal organization is but one, and perhaps no longer the most characteristic, creature populating today's organizational landscapes where trends such as financialization, digitalization or co-creation have turned organization into an increasingly 'unruly unit of analysis' (2014: 1225). They stress that organization theorists need to pay close attention to all of the newly emerging forms. Davis (2016) has already started on this endeavour, demonstrating that in the United States, the large-scale corporation is vanishing or becoming smaller. As it was those corporations that offered stable employment, well-paying jobs, pensions, and so on, the rise of the middle-class was presaged on their success and domination of the business landscape. Hence, his prediction from the new, digitally based, organizational forms is income inequality, work instability and the decline of the middle class. Bromley and Meyer (2015) take a somewhat different perspective. They examine global organizational expansion, what they call 'Hyper-Organization', and find the process of rationalization in the classic Weberian manner unbroken. As this process continues, they document the increasing multiplicity of stakeholders and the impact this has on organizational operation. Global expansion of the process of rationalization and the organizations it has brought about (Djelic and Quack, 2008; Höllerer, Walgenbach and Drori, 2017) and the expansion of its calculative principles to non-economic value spheres continue to be important issues in contemporary organizational research.

Digital innovation and digital transformation give rise to novel organizational forms with crowd-based platforms (Airbnb, Zoouniverse), product platforms (block chain) and digital building blocks (Wordpress, Upwork) (Srnicek, 2016; Hinings, Gegenhuber and Greenwood, 2018). This should inspire organization theorists to ask questions akin to the ones that the Industrial Revolution and the emergence of the complex, highly differentiated and bureaucratic organization sparked. Scholars have started to disentangle the multiplicity of business models and organizational forms, objectives and purposes, as well as the norms and values that the so-called sharing economy inheres (Oberg, Schöllhorn and Wruk, 2016; Kornberger et al., forthcoming). Intersectoral collaborations, many of them a new hope for addressing society's wicked problems, blur sector boundaries that served as classification for organizations (business organizations, not-for-profit organizations, public sector organizations) for many decades. Inspiration from the early organization researchers means asking questions such as the following: What are the new forms; what are their features and characteristics; what are the relationships of these novel forms to the classical bureaucratic organization and to one another?

This leads to another point that relates strongly to the starting points and foundations of organization theory: the value of comparative organizational analysis. The critiques of both bureaucracy and the one best way were founded on systematic comparative analysis. King, Felin and Whetten (2009: 4) state that comparative approaches 'were foundational ... (but have been) far less prominent in the past three decades'. Issues of novel organizational forms developing alongside the continued rationalization of non-business organizations, the rise of B-corps (companies certified for their commitment to standards of social and environmental performance, accountability and transparency). Along with issues of sustainability, income inequality, globalization, organizational wrongdoing, all call for systematic comparative analyses with the organization as the unit of analysis. Yet much contemporary research is dichotomized between qualitative, in-depth, single-case studies providing rich analysis of organizational processes, and large-scale databases that provide strong quantitative evidence but are usually highly schematic about the organizations concerned.

Allied to this is the other major interest of classical authors, namely, the relationship between organizations and society. In the early years of organization research, society was central as the soil in which organizations emerged. Later, it became truncated to 'everything outside the organization' and reduced to a handful of measurable variables. To take inspiration from the early times of organization theory also means to focus on the relationship between individual organizations as well as organizational forms with society in a broader way. What are the distinct societal developments that give rise to these novel forms? Technological developments (i.e. digitalization), ecological changes or changes in people's lifestyles (e.g. urbanization) are clearly highly relevant factors, but thinking of the ideational aspects Weber featured so prominently in his Protestant ethics, we need to ask what are the shifts in belief systems, values, the overall configuration of society that feed and are fed by these developments?

We continue to be an organizational society, but the organizational forms populating society are changing. We need to take seriously the recursive relationship between organizations and society. With the rise of new kinds of organizations, there are consequences for society. Organization theorists, again, can take note of the concerns of Marx, Weber, Michels, Selznick, Merton, Wright Mills and others who dealt with the ways in which organizations changed social institutions and the power, interests and values within those institutions.

We believe that the early history of organization theory is of interest for its own sake. But we also believe that there are contemporary lessons to be learned from the endeavours of those establishing our discipline between the 1860s and the 1960s. An understanding of our origins and starting points will affect our trajectory over the next 100 years!

References

Abbott, A. 1988. *The System of Professions*. Chicago: University of Chicago Press.

Adler, P. 2012. Marx and organization studies today. In P. Adler (ed.), *Oxford Handbook of Sociology and Organization Studies. Classical Foundations*. Oxford: Oxford University Press.

Adler, P. 2015. Marxist philosophy and organization studies: Marxist contributions to the understanding of some important organizational forms. *Research in the Sociology of Organizations*, 32: 123–153.

Adler, P. S., Kwon, S.-W. and Heckscher, C. 2008. Professional work: The emergence of collaborative community. *Organization Science*, 19: 359–376.

Albrow, M. 1970. *Bureaucracy*. London: Macmillan.

Alvesson, M. and Willmott, H. (eds.). 1992. *Critical Management Studies*. London: Sage.

Ansell, C. 2012. Mary Parker Follett and pragmatist organization. In P. Adler (ed.), *Oxford Handbook of Sociology and Organization Studies. Classical Foundations*. Oxford: Oxford University Press.

Augier, M. 2013. Behavioral theory of the firm: Hopes for the past; lessons from the future. *M@n@gement*, 16: 636–652.

Aviolo, B. and Yammarino, F. (eds.). 2013. *Transformation and Charismatic Leadership: The Road Ahead*. Bingley: Emerald Publishing.

Barnard, C. 1938. *The Functions of the Executive*. Cambridge, MA: Harvard University Press.

Barnard, C. 1948. *Organization and Management*. Cambridge, MA: Harvard University Press.

Battilana, J. and D'Aunno, T. 2009. Institutional work and the paradox of embedded agency. In T. Lawrence, R. Suddaby and B. Leca (eds.), *Institutional Work: Actors and Agency in Institutional Studies of Organizations*. Cambridge: Cambridge University Press.

Bendix, R. 1960. *Max Weber. An Intellectual Portrait*. Berkeley: University of California Press.

Benson, K. 1977. Organizations: A dialectical view. *Administrative Science Quarterly*, 4: 259–301.

Berger, M. 1956. Bureaucracy East and West. *Administrative Science Quarterly*, 1: 518–529.

Blau, P. 1955. *The Dynamics of Bureaucracy*. Chicago:University of Chicago Press.

Blau, P. 1956. *Bureaucracy in Modern Society*. New York: Random House.

Blau, P. 1964. *Exchange and Power in Social Life*. New York: Wiley.

Blau, P. and Schoenherr, R. 1971. *Formal Organizations*. New York: Basic Books.

Blau, P. and Scott, W. 1962. *Formal Organizations*. San Francisco: Chandler.

Boulding, K. 1953. *The Organizational Revolution*. New York: Harper.

Boulding, K. 1956. General systems theory: The skeleton of science. *Management Science*, 2: 197–208.

Braverman, H. 1974. *Labor and Monopoly Capital: The Degradation of Work in the Twentieth Century*. New York: Monthly Review Press.

Brech, E. 1969. *Management: Its Nature and Significance*. London: Pitman.

Brech, E., Thomson, A. and Wilson, J. 2010. *Lyndall Urwick, Management Pioneer: A Biography*. Oxford: Oxford Scholarship Online.

Bromley, P. and Meyer, J. 2015. *Hyper-organization: Global Organizational Expansion*. Oxford: Oxford University Press.

Brown, P. 1954. Bureaucracy in a government laboratory. *Social Forces*, 32: 259–268.

Burawoy, M. 1979. *Manufacturing Consent: Changes in the Labor Process under Monopoly Capitalism*. Chicago: University of Chicago Press.

Burnham, J. 1941. *The Managerial Revolution*. Harmondsworth: Penguin Books.

Burns, T. 1961. Micropolitics: Mechanisms of institutional change. *Administrative Science Quarterly*, 6: 257–281.

Burns, T. 1977. *The BBC: Public Service and Private World*. London: Macmillan.

Burns, T. and Stalker, G. M. 1961. *The Management of Innovation*. Oxford: Oxford University Press.

Burrell, G. and Morgan, G. 1979. *Sociological Paradigms and Organizational Analysis*. London: Heinemann.

Child, J. 1972. Organizational structure, environment and performance: The role of strategic choice. *Sociology*, 6: 1–22.

Clegg, S. and Dunkerley, D. 1980. *Organization, Class and Control*. London: Routledge and Kegan Paul.

Clegg, S. R. and Hardy, C. 2006. Some dare call it power. In S. R. Clegg, C. Hardy, T. B. Lawrence and W. R. Nord (eds.). 2006. *The SAGE Handbook of Organization Studies* (2nd ed.). London: Sage Publications.

Clegg, S. R., Hardy, C., Lawrence, T. B. and Nord, W. R. (eds.). 2006. *The SAGE Handbook of Organization Studies* (2nd ed.). London: Sage Publications.

Cohen, M., March, J. and Olsen, J. 1972. A garbage can model of organizational choice. *Administrative Science Quarterly*, 17: 1–25.

Crozier, M. 1964. *The Bureaucratic Phenomenon*. London: Tavistock.

Crozier, M. and Friedberg, E. 1977/1980. *Actors and Systems*. Chicago: University of Chicago Press.

Cyert, R. and March, J. 1963. *A Behavioral Theory of the Firm*. Englewood Cliffs, NJ: Prentice Hall.

Dahl, R. 1957. The concept of power. *Behavioral Science*, 2: 201–215.

Dalton, M. 1950. Conflicts between staff and line managerial officers. *American Sociological Review*, 15: 342–351.

Dalton, M. 1959. *Men Who Manage*. New York: John Wiley.

Davis, G. F. 2016. *The Vanishing American Corporation: Navigating the Hazards of a New Economy*. Oakland: Berrett-Koehler.

Davis, S. and Lawrence, P. 1977. *Matrix*. New York: Addison-Wesley.

Djelic, M. L. and Quack, S. 2008. Institutions and transnationalization. In R. Greenwood, C. Oliver, K. Sahlin and R. Suddaby (eds.), *The SAGE Handbook of Organizational Institutionalism*. Thousand Oaks, CA: Sage.

Djilas, M. 1957. *The New Class: An Analysis of the Communist System*. New York: Harcourt Brace Jovanovich.

Donaldson, L. 1995. *American Anti-management Theories of Organization*. Cambridge: Cambridge University Press.

Donaldson, L. 2001. *The Contingency Theory of Organization*. Thousand Oaks, CA: Sage.

Drucker, P. 1946. *The Concept of the Corporation*. New York: John Day.

du Gay, P. 2000. *In Praise of Bureaucracy: Weber, Organization, Ethics*. London: Sage.

Eisenstadt, S. 1958. Bureaucracy and bureaucratization. *Current Sociology*, 7: 99–164.

Emery, F. and Trist, E. 1965. The causal texture of organizational environments. *Human Relations*, 18: 21–32.

Emery, F. and Thorsrud, E. 1976. *Democracy at Work*. Leiden: Martinus Nijhoft.

Emirbayer, M. and Mische, A. 1998. What is agency? *American Journal of Sociology*, 103: 962–1023.

Espeland, W. N. and Stevens, M. L. 1998. Commensuration as a social process. *Annual Review of Sociology*, 24: 313–343.

Etzioni, A. 1961. *A Comparative Analysis of Complex Organizations*. New York: Free Press.

Etzioni, A. 1964. *Modern Organizations*. New York: The Free Press.

Fayol, H. 1916. *Administration industrielle et générale; prévoyance, organisation, commandement, coordination, controle*. Paris: H. Dunod et E. Pinat.

Fayol, H. 1949. *General and Industrial Management*. London: Pitman.

Follett, M. P. 1918. *The New State: Group Organization – the Solution for Popular Government*. New York: Longmans Green.

Follett, M. P. 1924. *Creative Experience*. London: Longman.

Follett, M. P. 1942. *Dynamic Administration*. New York: Harper.

Friedberg, E. 2009. Introduction. In M. Crozier, *The Bureaucratic Phenomenon*. London: Transaction Publishers.

Galbraith, J. 1973. *Designing Complex Organizations*. Reading, MA: Addison-Wesley.

Gavetti, G., Greve, H., Levinthal, D. and Ocasio, W. 2012. The behavioral theory of the firm: Assessment and prospects. *Academy of Management Annals*, 6: 1–40.

Gerth, H. 1952. The Nazi party: Its leadership and composition. In R. Merton, A. Gray, B. Hockey and H. Selvin (eds.), *Reader in Bureaucracy*. Glencoe, IL: The Free Press.

Gerth, H. H. and Mills, C. W. (eds.). 1946. *From Max Weber: Essays in Sociology*. London: Routledge and Kegan Paul.

Gouldner, A. 1954a. *Patterns of Industrial Bureaucracy*. Glencoe, IL: The Free Press.

Gouldner, A. 1954b. *Wildcat Strike*. Glencoe, IL: The Free Press.

Gouldner, A. 1957. Cosmopolitans and locals: Toward an analysis of latent social roles. *Administrative Science Quarterly*, 5: 485–521.

Gouldner, A. 1970. *The Coming Crisis of Western Sociology*. New York: Basic Books.

Greenwood, R. and Lawrence, T. 2005. The iron cage in the information age: The legacy and relevance of Max Weber for organization studies. *Organization Studies*, 26: 493–499.

Greenwood, R., Hinings, C. R. and Whetten, D. 2014. Rethinking institutions and organizations. *Journal of Management Studies*, 51: 1206–1220.

Greenwood, R., Oliver, C., Lawrence, T. and Meyer, R. E. (eds.). 2017. *The SAGE Handbook of Organizational Institutionalism* (2nd ed.). London: Sage Publications.

Gremion, P. 1992. Michel Crozier's long march: The making of the bureaucratic phenomenon. *Political Studies*, 40: 5–20.

Gulick, L. and Urwick, L. 1937. *Papers on the Science of Administration*. New York: Institute of Public Administration.

Hage, J. and Aiken, M. 1967a. Program change and organizational properties: A comparative analysis. *American Journal of Sociology*, 72: 503–519.

Hage, J. and Aiken, M. 1967b. Relationship of centralization to other structural properties. *Administrative Science Quarterly*, 12: 72–92.

Hage, J. and Aiken, M. 1969. Routine technology, social structure and organizational goals. *Administrative Science Quarterly*, 14: 366–376.

Hall, R. H. 1963a. The concept of bureaucracy: An empirical assessment. *American Journal of Sociology*, 69: 32–40.

Hall, R. H. 1963b. Bureaucracy and small organizations. *Sociology and Social Research*, 48: 38–46.

Hall, R. H. 1967. Some organizational considerations in the professional-organizational relationship. *Administrative Science Quarterly*, 12: 461–478.

Hall, R. H. 1968. Professionalization and bureaucratization. *American Sociological Review*, 33: 92–104.

Hall, R. H. (ed.). 1972. *The Formal Organization*. New York: Basic Books.

Hall, R. H., Haas, E. and Johnson, N. 1967. Organizational size, complexity, and formalization. *American Sociological Review*, 32: 903–912.

Hall, R. H. and Tittle, C. 1966. Bureaucracy and its correlates. *American Journal of Sociology*, 72: 267–272.

Hannan, M. and Freeman, J. 1977. The population ecology of organizations. *American Journal of Sociology*, 82: 929–964.

Hickson, D., Hinings, C. R., Schneck, R., Pennings, H. and Lee, C. 1971. A strategic contingencies theory of power. *Administrative Science Quarterly*, 16: 216–229.

Hickson, D. and McMillan, C. (eds.). 1981. *Organization and Nation: The Aston Programme IV*. Brookfield, VT: Gower Publishing.

Hinings, C. R., Gegenhuber, T. and Greenwood, R. 2018. Digital innovation and transformation: An institutional perspective. *Information and Organization*, 28 (1): 52–61.

Hinings, C. R. and Greenwood, R. 2015. Missing in action: The further contribution of Philip Selznick to contemporary institutional theory. *Research in the Sociology of Organization*, 44: 121–148.

Hinings, C. R. and Greenwood, R. 2017. The opening up of organization theory: Open systems, contingency theory, and organizational design. In A. Wilkinson, S. Armstrong and M. Lounsbury (eds.), *The Oxford Handbook of Management*. Oxford: Oxford University Press.

Hinings, C. R., Greenwood, R. and Meyer, R. E. 2018. Dusty books: The liability of oldness. *Academy of Management Review*, 43: 333–343.

Höllerer, M. A., Walgenbach, P. and Drori, G. S. 2017. The consequences of globalization for institutions and organizations. In R. Greenwood, C. Oliver, T. Lawrence and R. E. Meyer (eds.), *The SAGE Handbook of Organizational Institutionalism* (2nd ed.). London: Sage Publications.

Institute for Social Research. 2016. Timeline. Retrieved February 27, 2018, from http://home.isr.umich.edu/about/history/timeline/.

Jensen, M. and Meckling, W. 1976. Theory of the firm: Managerial behavior, agency costs, and ownership structure. *Journal of Financial Economics*, 3: 305–360.

Kast, F. and Rosenzweig, J. (eds.). 1973. *Contingency views of organization and management*. Palo Alto: Science Research Associates.

Katz, D. and Kahn, R. 1966. *The Social Psychology of Organizations*. New York: Wiley.

Kieser, A. and Kubicek, H. 1978a. *Organisationstheorien I: Wissenschaftstheoretische Anforderungen und kritische Analyse klassischer Ansätze*. Stuttgart: W. Kohlhammer.

Kieser, A. and Kubicek, H. 1978b. *Organisationstheorien II: Kritische Analysen neuer sozialwissenschaftlicher Ansätze*. Stuttgart: W. Kohlhammer.

Kieser, A. and Leiner, L. 2009. Why the rigour–relevance gap in management research is unbridgeable. *Journal of Management Studies*, 46: 516–533.

King, B., Felin, T. and Whetten, D. 2009. Comparative organizational analysis: An introduction. *Research in the Sociology of Organizations*, 26: 3–20.

Kipping, M. and Engwall, L. (eds.). 2002. *Management Consulting: Emergence and Dynamics of a Knowledge Industry*. New York: Oxford University Press.

Klein, L. 2010. Working with Joan Woodward. In N. Phillips, G. Sewell and D. Griffiths (eds.), *Research in the Sociology of Organizations*, 29: 35–40.

Knights, D. and Willmott, H. 1990. *Labour Process Theory*. London: Macmillan.

Kornberger, M., Justesen, L., Anders, K. M. and Mouritsen, J. (eds.). 2015. *Making Things Valuable*. Oxford: Oxford University Press.

Kornberger, M., Leixnering, S., Meyer, R. E. and Höllerer, M. forthcoming. Rethinking the Sharing Economy: The Nature and Organization of Sharing in the 2015 Refugee Crisis. *Academy of Management Discoveries*, 1–32.

Kornberger, M., Meyer, R. E., Brandtner, C. and Höllerer, M. 2017. When bureaucracy meets the crowd: Studying 'open government' in the Vienna City Administration. *Organization Studies*, 38: 179–200.

Kraatz, M. 2009. Leadership as institutional work: A bridge to the other side. In T. Lawrence, R. Suddaby and B. Leca (eds.), *Institutional Work*. Cambridge: Cambridge University Press.

Kraatz, M. 2015. Institutions and ideals: Philip Selznick's legacy for organizational studies. *Research in the Sociology of Organizations*, 44.

Kraatz, M. and Flores, R. 2015. Reinfusing values. *Research in the Sociology of Organizations*, 44: 353–381.

Küpper, W. and Ortmann, G. 1988. *Mikropolitik. Rationalität, Macht und Spiele in Organisationen*. Berlin: Opladen.

Landes, D. S. 1969. *The Unbound Prometheus: Technological Change and Industrial Development in Western Europe from 1750 to the Present*. Cambridge: Cambridge University Press.

Lawrence, P. and Lorsch, J. 1967a. *Organization and Environment: Managing Differentiation and Integration*. Cambridge, MA: Harvard University Graduate School of Business Administration.

Lawrence, P. and Lorsch, J. 1967b. Differentiation and integration in complex organizations. *Administrative Science Quarterly*, 12: 1–47.

Lawrence, P. and Lorsch, J. 1969. *Developing Organizations: Diagnosis and Action*. New York: Addison-Wesley.

Lenin, V. I. 1932. *The State and Revolution*. Moscow: International Publishing.

Lorsch, J. and Morse, J. 1974. *Organizations and Their Members: A Contingency Approach*. New York: Harper and Row.

Luhmann, N. 1964. *Funktionen und Folgen formaler Organisation*. Berlin: Duncker & Humblot.

Luhmann, N. 1968. *Zweckbegriff und Systemrationalität: Über die Funktion von Zwecken in sozialen Systemen*. Tübingen: J. C. B. Mohr.

Luhmann, N. 1984. *Soziale Systeme: Grundriß einer allgemeinen Theorie*. Frankfurt: Suhrkamp.

Mahoney, J. T. 2005. *Economic Foundations of Strategy*. Thousand Oaks, CA: Sage.

March, J. G. 1965. *Handbook of Organizations*. Chicago: Rand McNally.

March, J. and Olsen, J. 1989. *Rediscovering Institutions*. New York: Free Press.

March, J. and Simon, H. 1958. *Organizations*. New York: Wiley.

Martin, J. 2002. *Organizational Culture: Mapping the Terrain*. Thousand Oaks, CA: Sage.

Marx, K. 1852. *Der 18te Brumaire des Louis Napoleon*. New York: Die revolution.

Marx, K. 1867. *Das Kapital. Erster Band. Buch I: Der Produktionsprocess des Kapitals*. Hamburg: Verlag von Otto Meisner.

Marx, K. 1926. *The Eighteenth Brumaire of Louis Bonaparte*. London: Allen and Unwin.

Marx, K. 1932. *Die deutsche Ideologie*. Moscow: Marx-Engels Institute.

Marx, K. 1959. *Capital*. Moscow: Foreign Languages Publishing House.

Marx, K. 1965. *The German Ideology*. London: Lawrence and Wishart.

Marx, K. 1973. *Grundrisse: Foundations of a Critique of Political Economy*. London: Penguin Books.

Marx, K. and Engels, F. 1848. *Manifest der kommunistischen Partei*. London: Workers' Educational Association.

Marx, K. and Engels, F. 1955. *Manifesto of the Communist Party*. Moscow: Foreign Languages Publishing House.

Mayntz, R. 1963. *Soziologie der Organisation*. Berlin: Duncker & Humblot.

Mayntz, R. 1965. Max Webers Idealtypus der Bürokratie und die Organisationssoziologie. *Kölner Zeitschrift für Soziologie und Sozialpsychologie*, 17: 493–502.

Mayntz, R. 1968. *Bürokratische Organisation*. Neue Wissenschaftliche Bibliothek, Band 27. Köln: Kiepenhauer und Witsch.

Mayo, E. 1933. *The Human Problems of an Industrial Civilization*. London: Macmillan.

McKenna, C. 2006. *The World's Newest Profession: Management Consulting in the Twentieth Century*. Cambridge: Cambridge University Press.

Merton, R. 1936. The unanticipated consequences of purposive social action. *American Sociological Review*, 1: 894–904.

Merton, R. 1940. Bureaucratic structure and personality. *Social Forces*, 18: 560–568.

Merton, R. 1949. *Social Theory and Social Structure*. Glencoe, IL: The Free Press.

Merton, R. 1952. Bureaucratic structure and personality. In R. Merton, A. Gray, B. Hockey and H. Selvin (eds.), *Reader in Bureaucracy*. Glencoe, IL: The Free Press.

Merton, R., Gray, A., Hockey, B. and Selvin, H. (eds.). 1952. *Reader in Bureaucracy*. Glencoe, IL: The Free Press.

Metcalf, H. C. and Urwick, L. (eds.). 1941. *Dynamic Administration: The Collected Papers of Mary Parker Follett*. Bath: Management Publications Trust.

Meyer, R. E. 2008. New sociology of knowledge: Historical legacy and contributions to current debates in institutional research. In R. Greenwood, C. Oliver, K. Sahlin and R. Suddaby (eds.), *The SAGE Handbook of Organizational Institutionalism*. Thousand Oaks, CA: Sage.

Meyer, R. E. and Höllerer, M. 2014. Does institutional theory need redirecting? *Journal of Management Studies*, 51: 1221–1233.

Meyer, J. and Rowan, B. 1977. Institutionalized organizations: Formal structure as myth and ceremony. *American Journal of Sociology*, 83: 340–363.

Michels, R. 1911. *Zur Soziologie des Parteiwesens in der modernen Demokratie. Untersuchungen über die oligarchischen Tendenzen des Gruppenlebens*. Leipzig: Verlag von Dr. Werner Klinkhardt.

Michels, R. 1949. *Political Parties: A Sociological Study of the Oligarchical Tendencies of Modern Democracy.* Glencoe, IL: The Free Press.

Miller, D. and Le Breton-Miller, I. 2005. *Managing for the Long Run.* Cambridge, MA: Harvard Business School Press.

Mintzberg, H. 1979. *The Structuring of Organizations.* Englewood Cliffs, NJ: Prentice Hall.

Mouzelis, N. 1967. *Organization and Bureaucracy.* London: Routledge and Kegan Paul.

Oberg, A., Schöllhorn, T. and Wruk, D. 2016. How to measure similarities and differences of organizational forms in the Sharing Economy: A semantic network approach. European Group of Organization Studies Colloquium, Naples, Italy.

Parsons, T. 1951. *The Social System.* New York: The Free Press.

Parsons, T. 1956a. Suggestions for a sociological approach to the theory of organizations – I. *Administrative Science Quarterly,* 1: 63–85.

Parsons, T. 1956b. Suggestions for a sociological approach to the theory of organizations – II. *Administrative Science Quarterly,* 1: 224–239.

Parsons, T. 1960. *Structure and Process in Modern Society.* Glencoe, IL: Free Press.

Perrow, C. 1970. *Organizational Analysis: A Sociological View.* Belmont, CA: Wadsworth.

Perrow, C. 1972. *Complex Organizations: A Critical Essay.* Glenview, IL: Scott Foresman.

Pettigrew, A. 1985. *The Awakening Giant: Continuity and Change in ICI.* Oxford: Blackwell.

Pfeffer, J. and Salancik, G. 1978. *The External Control of Organizations: A Resource Dependence Perspective.* New York: Harper and Row.

Phillips, N., Sewell, G. and Griffiths, D. (eds.). 2010. Technology and organization: Essays in honour of Joan Woodward. *Research in the Sociology of Organizations,* 29.

Powell, W. and DiMaggio, P. (eds.). 1991. *The New Institutionalism in Organizational Analysis.* Chicago: University of Chicago Press.

Presthus, R. V. 1959. Behavior and bureaucracy in many cultures. *Public Administration Review,* 19: 25–35.

Presthus, R. V. 1961. Weberian v. welfare bureaucracy in a traditional society. *Administrative Science Quarterly,* 6: 1–24.

Presthus, R. V. 1962. *The Organizational Society.* New York: Knopf.

Pugh, D. S. (ed.). 1985. Organization theory. In *Selected Readings.* Harmondsworth: Penguin Books.

Pugh, D. and Hickson, D. (eds.). 1976. *Organization Structure in Its Context: The Aston Programme I*. Brookfield, VT: Gower Publishing.

Pugh, D. and Hickson, D. J. 2007. *Writers on Organizations*. London: Sage Publications.

Pugh, D. and Hinings, C. R. (eds.). 1976. *Organization Structure – Extensions and Peplications: The Aston Programme II*. Brookfield, VT: Gower Publishing.

Pugh, D. and Payne, R. (eds.). 1977. *Organization Behaviour in Its Context: The Aston Programme III*. Brookfield, VT: Gower Publishing.

Pugh, D., Hickson, D. J. and Hinings, C. R. 1964. *Writers on Organizations*. London: Hutchinson.

Pugh, D., Hickson, D. J., Hinings, C. R. and Turner, C. 1968. Dimensions of organization structure. *Administrative Science Quarterly*, 13: 65–105.

Pugh, D., Hickson, D. J. and Hinings, C. R. 1969a. An empirical taxonomy of structures of work organizations. *Administrative Science Quarterly*, 14: 115–126.

Pugh, D., Hickson, D. J., Hinings, C. R., McDonald, K., Turner, C. and Lupton, T. 1963. A conceptual scheme for organizational analysis. *Administrative Science Quarterly*, 8: 289–315.

Pugh, D., Hickson, D. J., Hinings, C. R. and Turner, C. 1969b. The context of organization structure. *Administrative Science Quarterly*, 14: 91–114.

Reay, T., Berta, W. and Kohn, M. 2009. What's the evidence on evidence-based management? *Academy of Management Perspectives*, 23: 5–18.

Rice, A. 1958. *Productivity and Social Organization*. London: Tavistock.

Roethlisberger, F. and Dickson, W. 1939. *Management and the Worker*. Cambridge, MA: Harvard University Press.

Rousseau, D. and McCarthy, S. 2007. Educating managers from an evidence-based perspective. *Academy of Management Learning & Education*, 6: 84–101.

Roy, D. 1952. Quota restriction and goldbricking in a machine shop. *American Journal of Sociology*, 57: 427–442.

Scott, W. R. and Davis, G. F. 2011. *Organizations and Organizing: Rational, Natural, and Open System Perspectives*. Upper Saddle River, NJ: Pearson Prentice Hall.

Selznick, P. 1943. An approach to the theory of bureaucracy. *American Sociological Review*, 8: 47–54.

Selznick, P. 1948. Foundations of the theory of organization. *American Sociological Review*, 13: 25–35.

Selznick, P. 1949. *TVA and the Grass Roots*. Berkeley, CA: University of California Press.

Selznick, P. 1952. *The Organizational Weapon*. New York: McGraw Hill.

Selznick, P. 1957. *Leadership in Administration*. New York: Harper and Row.

Selznick, P. 1996. Institutionalism 'old' and 'new'. *Administrative Science Quarterly*, 41: 270–277.

Shor, E. 1960. The Thai bureaucracy. *Administrative Science Quarterly*, 5: 66–86.

Silverman, D. 1970. *The Theory of Organizations: A Sociological Framework*. London: Heinemann.

Simon, H. 1947. *Administrative Behavior: A Study of Decision-Making Processes in Administrative Organization*. Glencoe: The Free Press.

Simon, H. 1957. *Administrative Behavior: A Study of Decision-Making Processes in Administrative Organization* (2nd ed.). New York: Macmillan.

Sine, W., Mitsuhashi, H. and Kirsch, D. 2006. Revisiting Burns and Stalker: Formal structure and new venture performance in emerging economic sectors. *Academy of Management Journal*, 49: 121–132.

Srnicek, N. 2016. *Platform Capitalism*. Cambridge: Polity Press.

Steyrer, J. 1998. Charisma and the archetypes of leadership. *Organization Studies*, 19: 807–828.

Stinchcombe, A. L. 1959. Bureaucratic and craft administration of production: A comparative study. *Administrative Science Quarterly*, 4: 168–187.

Svejenova, S., Croidieu, G. and Meyer, R. 2013. Welcome to the Hotel California: Strangers and hospitable organizations. *Nordiske Organisasjonsstudier*, 15: 68–90.

Taylor, F. W. 1903. *Shop Management*. New York: Harper.

Taylor, F. W. 1911. *The Principles of Scientific Management*. New York: Harper.

Taylor, F. W. 1947. *Scientific Management*. New York: Harper.

Thompson, J. 1957. Editorial. *Administrative Science Quarterly*, 1: 1–2.

Thompson, J. 1967. *Organizations in Action*. New York: McGraw Hill.

Trist, E. and Bamforth, K. 1951. Some social and psychological consequences of the Longwall method of coal-getting. *Human Relations*, 4: 3–28.

Udy, S. H. 1959. 'Bureaucracy' and 'rationality' in Weber's organization theory: An empirical study. *American Sociological Review*, 24: 791–795.

Urwick, L. 1944. *The Elements of Administration*. London: Pitman.

Urwick, L. 1952. *Notes on the Theory of Organization*. New York: American Management Association.

Urwick, L. 1956. *The Golden Book of Management: A Historical Record of the Life and Work of Seventy Pioneers*. Edited for the International Committee of Scientific Management. London: N. Neame.

Urwick, L. 1962. *A Short Survey of Industrial Management*. London: British Institute of Management.

Urwick, L. and Brech, E. 1950. *The Making of Scientific Management*. London: Pitman.

Van de Ven, A., Ganco, M. and Hinings, C. R. 2013. Returning to the frontier of contingency theory of organizational and institutional design. *Annals of the Academy of Management*, 7: 393–440.

Von Bertalanffy, L. (1956). General systems theory. In L. Von Bertalanffy and A. Rapoport (eds.), *General Systems: Yearbook of the Society for the Advancement of General Systems Theory, 1*. Washington, DC: Society for General Systems Research.

Waldo, D. 1948. *The Administrative State*. New York: Ronald Press Co.

Weber, M. 1921. *Gesammelte Aufsätze zur Religionssoziologie*. Tübingen: Mohr.

Weber, M. 1922. *Wirtschaft und Gesellschaft. Grundriß der verstehenden Soziologie*. Tübingen: Mohr.

Weber, M. 1924. *Gesammelte Aufsätze zur Soziologie und Sozialpolitik*. Tübingen: Mohr.

Weber, M. 1930. *The Protestant Ethic and the Spirit of Capitalism*. Glencoe, IL: The Free Press.

Weber, M. 1947. *The Theory of Social and Economic Organization*. Glencoe, IL: The Free Press.

Weber, M. 1963a. Objectivity in social science and social policy. In M. Natanson (ed.), *Philosophy of the Social Sciences*. New York: Random House.

Weber, M. 1963b. *The Sociology of Religion*. Boston: Beacon Press.

Weber, M. 1978. *Economy and Society*. Berkeley: University of California Press.

Weick, K. 1979. *The Social Psychology of Organizing*. Reading, MA: Addison-Wesley.

Whyte, W. H. 1956. *The Organization Man*. New York: Simon and Schuster.

Wiener, N. 1956. *I am a Mathematician*. New York: Doubleday.

Woodward, J. 1958. Management and technology. *Problems of Progress in Industry*, 3. London: HMSO.

Woodward, J. 1965. *Industrial Organization: Theory and Practice*. New York: Oxford University Press.

Woodward, J. (ed.). 1970. *Industrial Organization: Behaviour and Control*. Oxford: Oxford University Press.

Acknowledgements

We would like to thank Royston Greenwood for his encouragement, support, sage advice and editorial skills in the production of this Element.

Some of the material in this Element draws on previously published material:

Hinings, C. R. and Greenwood, R. 2015. Missing in action: The further contribution of Philip Selznick to contemporary institutional theory. *Research in the Sociology of Organization*, 44: 121–148.

Hinings, C. R. and Greenwood, R. 2017. The opening up of organization theory: Open systems, contingency theory, and organizational design. In A. Wilkinson, S. Armstrong and M. Lounsbury (eds.), *The Oxford Handbook of Management*. Oxford: Oxford University Press.

Hinings, C. R., Greenwood, R. and Meyer, R. E. 2018. Dusty books: The liability of oldness. *Academy of Management Review*, 43(2).

Cambridge Elements ☰

Organization Theory

Nelson Phillips
Imperial College London
Nelson Phillips is the Abu Dhabi Chamber Professor of Strategy and Innovation at Imperial College London. His research interests include organization theory, technology strategy, innovation and entrepreneurship, often studied from an institutional theory perspective.

Royston Greenwood
University of Alberta
Royston Greenwood is the Telus Professor of Strategic Management at the University of Alberta, a Visiting Professor at the University of Cambridge and a Visiting Professor at the University of Edinburgh. His research interests include organizational change and professional misconduct.

About the Series
Organization theory covers many different approaches to understanding organizations. Its focus is on what constitutes the how and why of organizations and organizing, bringing understanding of organizations in a holistic way. The purpose of *Elements in Organization Theory* is to systematize and contribute to our understanding of organizations.

Cambridge Elements $\equiv$

Organization Theory

Elements in the Series

Printed in the United States
By Bookmasters